Assessment of Contaminant Exposure and Effects on Ospreys Nesting along the Lower Duwamish River, Washington, 2006–07

By Branden L. Johnson, Charles J. Henny, and James L. Kaiser, U.S. Geological Survey, Jay W. Davis, U.S. Fish and Wildlife Service, and Edmund P. Schulz, U.S. Geological Survey

Open-File Report 2009-1255

U.S. Department of the Interior
U.S. Geological Survey

U.S. Department of the Interior
KEN SALAZAR, Secretary

U.S. Geological Survey
Marcia K. McNutt, Director

U.S. Geological Survey, Reston, Virginia: 2009

For more information on the USGS—the Federal source for science about the Earth, its natural and
living resources, natural hazards, and the environment, visit http://www.usgs.gov or call 1-888-ASK-USGS.
For an overview of USGS information products, including maps, imagery, and publications,
visit *http://www.usgs.gov/pubprod*

To order this and other USGS information products, visit *http://store.usgs.gov*

Suggested citation:
Johnson, B.L., Henny, C.J., Kaiser, J.L., Davis, J.W., and Schulz, E.P., 2009, Assessment of contaminant exposure
and effects on Ospreys nesting along the Lower Duwamish River, Washington, 2006–07: U.S Geological Survey
Open-File Report 2009-1255, 88 p.

Contents

Figures

Tables

Conversion Factors and Datum

Multiply		By	To obtain
		Volume	
albumin (ALB)	g/dL	10	g/L
pre-albumin (preALB)	g/dL	10	g/L
alpha 1globulins (α1G)	g/dL	10	g/L
alpha 2 globulins (α2G)	g/dL	10	g/L
beta globulins (βG)	g/dL	10	g/L
gamma globulins (γG)	g/dL	10	g/L
total plasma protein (TPP)	g/dL	10	g/L
amylase (AMYL)	IU/L	1.0	U/L
blood urea nitrogen (BUN)	mg/dL	0.357	mmol/L
creatinine (CREA)	mg/dL	88.4	μmol/L
calcium (Ca)	mg/dL	0.25	mmol/L
cholesterol (CHOL)	mg/dL	0.02586	mmol/L
glucose (GLUC)	mg/dL	0.05551	mmol/L
lipase (LI)	IU/L	1.0	U/L
phosphorus (PHOS)	mg/dL	0.323	mmol/L
triglycerides (TRIG)	mg/dL	0.01129	mmol/L
uric acid (UA)	mmol/L	0.0168	mg/dL
potassium (K)	mmol/L	1.0	mEg/L
sodium (Na)	mmol/L	1.0	mEg/L
thyroxine (T4)	μg/dL	12.87	nmol/L
alkaline phosphatase (Alk Phos)	IU/L	1.0	U/L
alanine aminotransferase (ALT)	IU/L	1.0	U/L
aspartate aminotransferase (AST)	IU/L	1.0	U/L
butyrylcholinesterase (BCHE)	IU/L	1.0	U/L
creatine kinase (CK)	IU/L	1.0	U/L
gamma-glutamyl transferase (GGT)	IU/L	1.0	U/L
glutathione reductase (GSSGred)	IU/L	1.0	U/L
lactate dehydrogenase (LDH)	IU/L	1.0	U/L
lactate dehydrogenase-L (LDH-L)	IU/L	1.0	U/L
selenium-dependent glutathione peroxidase (S-GSHpx)	IU/L	1.0	U/L
total glutathione peroxidase (T-GSHpx)	IU/L	1.0	U/L
		Length	
kilometer (km)		0.6214	mile (mi)
meter (m)		3.281	foot (ft)

Additional Units

ft^3/s	cubic feet per second
m^3/s	cubic meters per second
ga	gauge, refers to size of needle
mEq	milliequivalents
mL	milliliter
µL	microliter
g/dL	grams per deciliter
mg/dL	milligrams per deciliter
mmol/L	millimoles per liter
µmol/L	micromoles per liter
nmol/L	nanomoles per liter
IU/L	International units per liter
U/L	units per liter
g	gravity - refers to the relative centrifugal force, the measurement of acceleration applied to a sample within a centrifuge
v/v	percent volume in volume, this defines milliliters of a constituent in 100 mL of a preparation

Concentrations of chemical contaminants in osprey tissues are given in milligrams per kilograms wet weight (mg/kg ww), milligrams per kilogram dry weight (mg/kg dw), micrograms per kilogram wet weight (µg/kg ww), or nanograms per kilogram wet weight (ng/kg ww).

Concentration reported	Are equivalent to	
mg/kg	micograms per gram (µg/g)	parts per million (ppm)
µg/kg	nanograms per gram (ng/g)	parts per billion (ppb)
ng/kg	picograms per gram (pg/g)	parts per trillion (ppt)
1 ppm	1,000 ppb	1,000,000 ppt
1 ppb	0.001 ppm	1,000 ppt
1 ppt	0.000001 ppm	0.001 ppb

List of Acronyms

α1G	alpha 1 globulins
α2G	alpha 2 globulins
βG	beta globulins
γG	gamma globulins
ΣPBDEs	sum polybrominated diphenyl ether congeners
ΣPCBs	sum polychlorinated biphenyl congeners
2,4-D	2,4-dichlorophenoxyacetic acid
2,4-DB	4-2,4-dichlorophenoxy butyric acid
2,4,5-T	2,4,5 trichlorophenoxy acetic acid
112	S. 112 St., osprey nest site (RM 5.7)
AGR	albumin/globulin ratio
ALB	albumin

AlkPhos	alkaline phosphatase
ALT	alanine aminotransferase
AMYL	amylase
AST	aspartate aminotransferase
BC	British Columbia
BCR	blood urea nitrogen/creatinine ratio
BDC	Boeing Development Center, osprey nest site (RM 4.9)
BMF	biomagnification factors
BCHE	butyrylcholinesterase
BUN	blood urea nitrogen
Ca	calcium
CHOL	cholesterol
CK	creatine kinase
CM	carps and minnows
CMP	Cecil Moses Memorial Park, osprey nest site (RM 5.7)
CO_2	carbon dioxide
CPK	creatine phosphokinase
CREA	creatinine
CSG	Cadman Sand and Gravel, osprey nest site (RM 1.0)
CVAFS	cold vapor atomic fluorescence spectrometry
DDD	1,1-dichloro-2,2-bis(p-chlorophenyl)ethane
DDE	1,1-dichloro-2,2-bis(p-chlorophenyl)ethylene
DDT	1,1,1-trichloro-2,2-bis(p-chlorophenyl)ethane
Di-TCP	dimethyl-TCP
dw	dry weight
EB	Elliott Bay
EC-GC	electron-capture gas chromatograph
ECNI	electron capture negative ionization
ECOSS	Environmental Coalition of South Seattle
EH	Everett Harbor
EPA	Environmental Protection Agency
GC/MS	gas chromatography/mass spectrometry
GGT	gamma-glutamyl transpeptidase
GLIER	Great Lakes Institute for Environmental Research
GLM	general linear models
GLU	glucose
GSH	glutathione
GSSGred	glutathione reductase
HBCD	hexabromocyclododecane
HC	Hamm Creek, Seattle City Light Substation, osprey nest site (RM 4.4)
HCB	hexachlorobenzene
H6CDD	hexachlorodibenzo-p-dioxin
H7CDD	heptachlorodibenzo-p-dioxin
H6CDF	hexachlorodibenzofuran
H7CDF	heptachlorodibenzofuran
HCH	hexachlorocyclohexane (α, β, and γ fractions)
HE	heptachlor epoxide

Hg	mercury
K	potassium
LCP	Lafarge Cement Plant, osprey nest site (RM 1.0)
LDH	lactate dehydrogenase
LDH-L	lactate dehydrogenase-L
LDR	lower Duwamish River
LDW	Lower Duwamish Waterway
LI	lipase
LW	Lake Washington
MCPA	2-methyl-4-chlorophenoxyacetic acid
MS	mass spectrometer
Na	sodium
NWRC	National Wildlife Research Centre
OCs	organochlorines
OCDD	octachlorodibenzo-p-dioxin
OCDF	octachlorodibenzofuran
OCS	octachlorostyrene
PAHs	polycyclic aromatic hydrocarbons
PBDEs	polybrominated diphenyl ethers
PCBs	polychlorinated biphenyls
PCDD	polychlorinated dibenzo-p-dioxin
P5CDD	pentachlorodibenzo-p-dioxin
PCDF	polychlorinated dibenzofuran
P5CDF	pentachlorodibenzofuran
PHOS	phosphorus
preALB	prealbumin
PS	Puget Sound
PWRC	Patuxent Wildlife Research Center
QCB	pentachlorobenzene
REF	righteye flounders
RIA	radioimmunoassay
RI/FS	remedial investigation and feasibility study
Rkm	river kilometer
RM	river mile
RRF	relative response factor
S-GSHpx	selenium-dependent glutathione peroxidase
SRE	Snohomish River Estuary
T4	thyroxine
T5	Terminal 5, osprey nest site (RM 0.0)
T18	Terminal 18, osprey nest site (RM 0.0)
T104	Terminal 104, Seattle Transload, osprey nest site (RM 0.1)
T105	Terminal 105, Nucor Steel Recycling Yard, osprey nest site (RM 0.4)
T115	Terminal 115, Northland Services, osprey nest site (RM 1.5)
TBA	total bile acids
TCB	tetrachlorobenzene
TCDD	tetrachlorodibenzo-p-dioxin
TCDF	tetrachlorodibenzofuran

TCT	Tukwila cell tower, osprey nest site
TEF	toxic equivalency factor
TEQ	2,3,7,8-TCDD-toxic equivalent concentration
T-GSHpx	total glutathione peroxidase
TL	tail length
TotChlor	total chlordanes
TPP	total plasma protein
TRIG	triglycerides
UA	uric acid
UMCPL	University of Miami School of Medicine Comparative Pathology Laboratory
UNK	unknown
USEPA	U.S. Environmental Protection Agency
USFWS	U.S. Fish and Wildlife Service
USGS	U.S. Geological Survey
WBC	white blood cells
WDFW	Washington Department of Fish and Wildlife
WR	Willamette River
ww	wet weight

Assessment of Contaminant Exposure and Effects on Ospreys Nesting along the Lower Duwamish River, Washington, 2006–07

By Branden L. Johnson[1], Charles J. Henny[1], James L. Kaiser[1], Jay W. Davis[2], and Edmund P. Schulz[3]

Abstract

We evaluated the effects of contaminants on osprey (*Pandion haliaetus*) nesting along the lower Duwamish River (LDR), Washington, and used the upper reach of the Willamette River (WR), Oregon, as a reference site. Osprey eggs and nestling blood (plasma) were collected at nests along the LDR (11 eggs, 7 plasmas) and WR (10 eggs, 6 plasmas) in 2006–07 and analyzed for contaminants. Additionally, hematology and serum chemistries were determined in the blood/plasma samples of nestlings (about 35–45 days old) and were used as potential indicators of stress induced by contaminant exposure. Detailed foraging information for ospreys nesting along the LDR was collected and evaluated to better understand contaminant profiles observed in the eggs and plasma. Additional residue data from 26 osprey eggs collected and analyzed in 2002–03 from nests along the LDR, Snohomish River Estuary (SRE) and Lake Washington (LW) in the Puget Sound (PS) region also were evaluated.

Ospreys nesting along the LDR in 2006–07 primarily ate hatchery-reared salmonids (*Salmonidae*; age 1 year) (usually *Oncorhynchus spp.*) (61.0% incidence [57.1% biomass]) captured in the LDR during the pre-incubation (before egg laying) period (N = 213). The diet then changed. Righteye flounders (*Pleuronectidae*) (primarily soles) (30.5% [28.0% biomass]) captured in the PS, carps and minnows (*Cyprinidae*) (primarily peamouth) (21.5% [19.3% biomass]) captured in LW, and salmonids (age 2–3+ year) (18.0% [34.4% biomass]) primarily captured in Elliott Bay/PS characterized the diet of ospreys during the nestling period (N = 249). The diet of ospreys nesting along the WR (based on previous investigations) was predominantly comprised of largescale suckers (*Catostomus macrocheilus*) (>68% [>82% biomass]).

The sum of polychlorinated biphenyl congener (ΣPCB) residues were significantly higher in the 2006–07 LDR osprey eggs (geometric means, 897 micrograms per kilogram weight wet [μg/kg ww]) and in the plasma of nestlings (40 μg/kg ww) than in WR osprey eggs and nestling plasma (eggs: 182 μg/kg ww; plasma: 7 μg/kg ww; eggs and plasma $P < 0.0001$). The sum of polybrominated diphenyl ether (ΣPBDE) concentrations were significantly lower in LDR tissue samples compared to WR osprey eggs and plasma (eggs: LDR = 321 μg/kg ww, WR = 897 μg/kg ww, $P = 0.0003$; plasma: LDR = 6 μg/kg ww, WR = 22 μg/kg ww, $P = 0.003$).

[1] U.S. Geological Survey, Forest and Rangeland Ecosystem Science Center, Corvallis, Oregon.
[2] U.S. Fish and Wildlife Service, Washington Fish and Wildlife Office, Lacey, Washington.
[3] Consulting Biologist (USGS Contractor), Everett, Washington.

Numerous hematological (hematocrit, eosinophils, heterophils) and biochemical (total glutathione peroxidase, selenium-dependent glutathione peroxidase, aspartate aminotransferase, uric acid, glucose, total plasma protein, potassium, albumin-globulin ratio, prealbumin, beta globulin and gamma globulin) determinations were significantly different between LDR and WR nestlings. Several significant relationships between contaminant groups and histological parameters were observed, although caution is required with interpretation of these data because sample size was low.

ΣPCB concentrations in LDR osprey eggs decreased by 53% since 2003 (P = 0.0157), in addition to most organochlorine (OC) pesticides (HCB, TotChlor, b-HCH, DDT, DDE, DDD, HE, and dieldrin). Total mercury concentrations in LDR osprey eggs decreased between 2003 and 2007 (P = 0.0453); and the difference in mean ΣPBDEs in eggs between 2003 and 2006–07 was not significant (P = 0.1992). Organochlorine pesticides (QCB, HCB, OCS, mirex, HE, dieldrin), ΣPCB and coplanar PCBs (77, 81, 126, 169), most dioxins and furans, and ΣPBDE residues were higher in osprey eggs collected from nests adjacent to LW than eggs collected from the SRE and LDR study areas in 2002–03. Although four nests at the mouth of the LDR failed in 2006 (four of nine nests studied), two of which again failed in 2007, concentrations of the contaminants analyzed in eggs collected at nests that failed were less than known effect levels. Osprey egg residue concentrations reflect the osprey diet during the pre-egg laying stage, which for LDR birds included a high percentage of relatively clean recently released hatchery-reared salmonids. Thus, the osprey contaminant burdens observed in eggs were not reflective of local conditions.

Other contaminants not measured in this study and/or the additive or synergistic effect of contaminants may have contributed to the observed reproductive failure at several nests as well as the changes in observed hematology and serum chemistry determinations. Although some of the blood/plasma data suggest that the nestlings from the LDR may be immunologically compromised, further study is warranted with a larger dataset. Observed differences in hematological and biochemical determinations between rivers are difficult to interpret because baseline reference data are not available for osprey. Further investigations are necessary to determine the key factors driving the observed cellular differences and to assess the biological significance of these determinations.

Introduction

The Lower Duwamish Waterway (LDW) Superfund Site is an 8.7 km (5.4 mi) industrialized estuary of the LDR, Washington, with sediment contaminated from years of industrial activity and stormwater runoff. Chemicals of potential concern in the LDW are polychlorinated biphenyls (PCBs), trace metals (particularly arsenic), tributyltins, semi-volatiles, polycyclic aromatic hydrocarbons (PAHs), and dioxins and furans. Besides a study that evaluated dioxin-like chlorobiphenyls in five great blue heron (*Ardea herodias*) eggs (Krausmann, 2002), studies assessing injuries to wildlife species at the LDW site have been limited and have predominantly involved fish. Injuries associated with contaminant burdens in fish identified in previous studies include fin erosions, tumors, reproductive and behavioral alterations, suppressed disease resistance, and reduced populations (Arkoosh and others, 1991, 1998; Myers and others, 1991, 2003; Johnson and others, 1998, 2002; Meador and others, 2002). Ospreys (*Pandion haliaetus*) began nesting along the LDR in the early 1990s (U.S. Geological Survey, unpub. data) and provided a new resource for monitoring contaminants in this system and assessing their potential effects on an avian species.

Ospreys have many positive characteristics for biomonitoring including:
- a cosmopolitan distribution,
- a diet at the top of food web that consists almost exclusively of fish,
- high nest site fidelity and forage near their nest sites,
- sensitive to DDE-induced eggshell thinning,
- widely studied for other chlorinated hydrocarbon and mercury pollutant effects (Poole, 1989; Elliott and others, 1998, 2000; Henny and others, 2003).

Osprey eggs have been routinely sampled for monitoring contaminants in large rivers, bays, and estuaries (Wiemeyer and others, 1988; Bowerman and others, 1995; Elliott and others, 1998, 2000, 2001; Henny and others, 2003, 2004, 2008, 2009a; Martin and others, 2003; Rattner and others, 2004; Toschik and others, 2005; de Solla and Martin, 2009); and several osprey studies have incorporated sampling the blood of young as a way to monitor contaminants (Elliott and others, 1998; Martin and others, 2003; Rattner and others, 2008; de Solla and Martin, 2009). Blood sampling (for cellular determinations) also has been used as a health monitoring tool for wild avian species (Dawson and Bortolotti, 1997; Mealey and others, 2004). Evaluating hematological and biochemical determinations to assess the health of free-living birds is an ideal nondestructive tool for monitoring the health of aquatic systems as cellular evaluations can be useful for diagnosing avian diseases (Bierer and others, 1963; Campbell and Dein, 1984) and for potentially determining the effects of chronic, low-level, sub-lethal exposure to environmental toxicants, which has proven useful in the management of white-tailed deer (*Odocoileus virginianus leucurus*) (Redig and others, 1983).

PCBs are of particular concern in the LDW as high concentrations have been found in water, sediments, and fish (Malins and others, 1984, 1987; O'Neill and others, 1998; Windward, 2003; Johnson and others, 2007). Recently a complete ecological risk assessment found that PCBs are the contaminant that poses the greatest risk to wildlife (Windward, 2007a). PCBs can reach concentrations in avian adults and eggs that may cause toxic effects (Hoffman and others, 1998b; Fernie and others, 2001a). Toxic effects, which in adults are contingent on species, dosage, PCB congener composition, and the birds' physiology, include mortality, deformities, decreased body weight, reproductive impairment, edema, porphyria and other physiological and immunological impairment (Barron and others, 1995; Eisler and Belisle, 1996; Hoffman and others, 1996a, 1996b, 1998b; Eisler, 2000; Fernie and others, 2001a; Custer and others, 2003). In addition to reproductive impairment, PCB exposure has been associated with altered reproductive behavior described by increased time spent in the courtship phase, reduced pair bond formation, nests built of poor quality, delayed nest building, delayed egg laying, eggs buried in the nest material, decreased nest attentiveness including inconsistent incubation, and increased nest abandonment (Peakall and Peakall, 1973; Tori and Peterle, 1983; Arena and others, 1999; McCarty and Secord, 1999a, 1999b; Fernie and others, 2001a). Avian eggs contaminated with PCBs have been associated with decreased hatching success, delayed hatching, increased embryonic deformities, arrested lymphoid development, edema, liver lesions, decreased organ weights, and reduced growth and survival (Bush and others, 1974; Hill and others, 1975; Haseltine and Prouty, 1980; Brunstorm and Reutergardh, 1986; Hoffman and others, 1986; Brunstorm, 1989; Gilbertson and others, 1991; Yamashita and others, 1993; Bosveld and Van den Berg, 1994; Barron and others, 1995; Bosveld and others, 1995; Larson and others, 1996; Hoffman and others, 1998b; Powell and others, 1998; McCarty and Secord, 1999a, 1999b; Fernie and others, 2001a; Custer and others, 2003).

Extensive surveys were conducted by boat and car in 2002 to assess the occurrence and distribution of ospreys nesting along and adjacent to the Duwamish River and shoreline areas of LW and the Central Puget Sound (PS) near Seattle, Washington. Surveys were conducted following the collection of eggs from 12 osprey and 12 cormorant nests located on overwater pilings in the Snohomish River Estuary (SRE) near Everett, Washington, in 2002. Eggs from newly located nests along the LDR (N = 7), LW (N = 3), and SRE (N = 4) study sites also were collected in 2003. All egg samples were analyzed for congener-specific PCBs, organochlorine (OC) pesticides, polybrominated diphenyl ethers (PBDEs), herbicides, and fungicides (see section, "Results"). To better understand residue concentrations in eggs collected from LDR osprey nests in 2003, a more comprehensive study was conducted in 2006–07 with this population and included detailed foraging observations and the collection of additional osprey eggs as well as blood/plasma samples from advanced-age nestlings.

Study objectives were:

1. Determine productivity of selected osprey nests along the LDR and WR;

2. Assess the dietary habits of ospreys nesting along the LDR by evaluating prey species delivered to nests (via direct observation and photographic record) to determine percent contributions of each fish species to the overall diet (particularly during the critical nesting periods: pre-egg laying [pre-incubation] and nestling periods), and to identify fish capture locations to better understand contaminant profiles in osprey eggs and nestling blood;

3. Assess contaminant exposure to ospreys nesting along the Duwamish River by collecting and analyzing osprey eggs for congener-specific PCBs, OC pesticides, PBDEs, herbicides, fungicides, and total mercury (Hg);

4. Assess geographical differences in contaminant residues measured in osprey from the LDR, WR and other selected sites in the Puget Sound;

5. Evaluate temporal differences in contaminant residues in LDR osprey;

6. Assess contaminant exposure to osprey nestlings by collecting and analyzing blood plasma for the same aforementioned contaminants, as well as mercury by collecting and analyzing nestling feathers;

7. Assess overall condition (health) of osprey nestlings by evaluating hematological and biochemical determinations;

8. Evaluate associations, if any, among contaminants and hematological and biochemical parameters in nestling blood plasma;

9. Determine contaminant concentrations and examine residue patterns in selected prey fish species collected from osprey foraging locations; and

10. Evaluate the current contaminant concentrations as well as physiological and histological parameters to assess possible adverse effects on osprey productivity.

Materials and Methods

Study Area

The Duwamish River flows northwest for approximately 19 river kilometers (RKM) (12 river miles [RM]) from the confluence of the Green River and the former confluence of the Black River near Tukwila, Washington, to the southern end of Harbor Island near downtown Seattle where it divides forming the East and West Waterways before discharging into Elliott Bay (EB) (fig. 1). Annual discharge from the river was 43 to 51 m^3/s (2,300 to 2,350 ft^3/s) measured at the Tukwila USGS gaging station (12113350). The LDR study area includes the East and West Waterways, Harbor Island to Turning Basin 3, and upstream to RKM 10.5 (RM 6.5). The LDW is an 8.7 RKM (5.4 RM) industrialized estuary of the LDR; this river segment does not include the East and West Waterways. The LDW has been extensively dredged, filled and channelized to facilitate navigation and utilized for industrial and commercial development over the last 100 years resulting in numerous outfalls (including storm drains and combined sewer overflows) that currently discharge into the river. Historical and current industrial and commercial operations include cargo handling and storage, metal and paper fabrication, wood preservation, petroleum storage, food processing, marine construction, boat/ship manufacturing, airplane parts manufacturing, and other general manufacturing (U.S. Environmental Protection Agency, 2001; Windward, 2003). The river is contained within a hardened shoreline consisting of bulkheads, riprap, and docks and ranges in width from 152 to 305 m (500–1000 ft) in the lower reach to 46–61 m (150–200 ft) upstream (Windward, 2003). The LDW was added as a Superfund Site to the U.S. Environmental Protection Agency's (EPA) National Priority List of the Nation's most contaminated hazardous waste sites in 2001. PCBs, trace metals, tributyltins, semi-volatiles, PAHs, dioxins, and furans have been identified as chemicals of potential concern. Probable contaminant sources are thought to include historical land use and disposal practices, industrial or municipal releases (including both permitted and unpermitted wastewater and stormwater discharges), spills or leaks, atmospheric deposition, and waste disposal either on land or in landfills (Windward, 2003). Numerous cleanup efforts are occurring and/or planned in the LDR river section selected for this study. Assessment of potential injury to osprey was not part of the remedial investigation (RI) (completed in 2007) required by EPA Superfund regulations, but provides baseline information on birds nesting along the LDR.

The river and estuary support an anadromous fishery, migratory birds, and four federally listed species (chinook salmon [*Oncorhynchus tshawytscha*], coho salmon [*Oncorhynchus kisutch*], steelhead trout [*Oncorhynchus mykiss*], bull trout [*Salvelinus confluentus*]. This system further provides fish for recreational, commercial, and subsistence purposes; the Duwamish River is part of the traditional fishing grounds for the Muckleshoot and Suquamish Indian Tribes. Initiated in 1901, the Green-Duwamish River supports one of the oldest and most productive salmon hatchery programs in PS and annually releases approximately 10 million juvenile salmon (primarily chinook) from three salmon hatcheries along the river system (Anchor Environmental, 2005). In 1983, the fishery program began raising chinook salmon for a year (15 months of age) at the Icy Creek Rearing Ponds rather than the usual 90 days prior to their release to contribute to the "blackmouth" (immature chinook salmon) fishery in PS. Chinook raised for longer periods tend to remain and mature in the PS rather than migrating to distant northern ocean waters to mature (Jim Shannon, Senior Scientist, David Evans and Associates Inc., oral commun., 2007). Approximately 300,000 fish are released each April from the pond into the Green/Duwamish River (National Marine Fisheries Service, 2002).

Duwamish River osprey nests monitored for this study (2006–07) were selected from sites along the LDR (N = 9, RKM 0.0–10.5 [RM 0.0–6.5]) (fig. 1). The upper mainstem Willamette River (WR) between Newberg and Harrisburg, Oregon, was chosen as a reference area and nests (N = 10) were strategically selected from river sections (RKM 98–254 [RM 61–158]) where eggs of osprey nesting along this river segment were known to contain low PCB residue concentrations in 2001 (fig. 1). This osprey population has been studied for many years (Henny and Kaiser, 1996; Henny and others, 2003, 2009a) and a great deal of baseline information is known about the population, its food habits, and contaminant loads in both fish and osprey eggs.

Osprey Foraging and Nesting Observations

Foraging and nesting behaviors of osprey at LDR study site nests were monitored 2–3 times per week during the nesting period (2006: April 4 to August 21; 2007: April 2 to August 9). Nest activity at WR reference nests were monitored weekly in 2006 (May–August) and on one occasion in 2007 (July 20) to determine number of young produced (eggs were not collected from WR osprey nests in 2007). Nesting behavior observations (stand, incubate, brood/shade, tend) were recorded and reproductive success determined following definitions in Postupalsky (1974, 1977). Nest productivity was determined by counting the number of nestlings raised to fledge age (about 55 days). Productivity also was monitored at nests where eggs were collected in 2003 (LDR, N = 7; LW, N = 3; SRE, N = 4). Intensive foraging observations were not conducted at the WR reference sites concurrent with this study, but were based on previously collected dietary data (Henny and others, 2003; Johnson and others, 2008). Foraging behavior observations on the LDR were systematically conducted on a daily basis, primarily in the early morning hours at each nest and were concentrated during the pre-egg laying and nestling periods (observations were conducted opportunistically during the incubation and fledgling periods) to identify foraging and prey capture locations and prey species delivered to nests. Breeding chronology was determined for each nest by conducting distant observations using binoculars and telescopes to confirm the presence of an incubating bird or of young. Estimates of egg-laying and fledge dates were verified by back-calculating or extrapolating from estimates of embryo development in the sample eggs collected for contaminant analysis based on a 38-day incubation period and 55-day fledge age (Stotts and Henny, 1975). Prey fish were identified to family (genus and species when possible) by examining photographic records (images) of prey delivered to nest sites, which were taken using cameras equipped with 300–500 mm zoom lenses. Prey fish size (total length [TL]) was visually estimated in relation to osprey tail length (mean value for adult male = 205 mm) (Macnamara, 1972). The location (waterbody) of each osprey fish capture was determined by recording the cardinal direction of the foraging bird's departure and return flight to the nest with the prey fish or by the specific fish capture location. When the departure and return flight differed, the fish capture location was recorded based on the location of the return flight direction. Assumed but unknown feeding locations were supported by the fact that peamouth (*Mylocheilus caurinus*) spawn in LW as opposed to the LDR or PS; and English sole (*Pleuronectes vetulus*) are predominantly found in PS, are not common in the LDR, and are not found in LW (Jim Shannon, Senior Scientist, David Evans and Associates Inc., oral commun., 2007). Fish-capture locations for osprey nesting on the LDR were grouped according to the following water bodies: LDR, EB/PS (hereafter referred to PS), LW, and unknown (UNK) (fig. 1).

Osprey Tissue Sampling

Osprey Eggs

A random, partially incubated egg was collected from 7 LDR nests and from 10 WR nests in 2006 using the sample egg technique (Blus and others, 1984) (fig. 1). In 2007, eggs were collected from four LDR nests: three nests that failed in 2006 and one nest that contained two addled eggs (one was analyzed) on the day of blood collection. Residue data from eggs collected from 26 nests in 2002–03 (2002 N: SRE, 12; 2003 N: LDR, 7; LW, 3; SRE, 4) also are reported. All 31 egg samples were processed according to the U.S. Fish and Wildlife Service's *Protocol for Avian Egg Collection and Removal of Contents for Contaminant Analysis* (Hudson River Natural Resource Trustees, 2004). Egg development was estimated based on embryo development (Bird and others, 1984; with modifications by Charles J. Henny). Egg contents were placed into chemically cleaned glass jars and stored frozen ($-20°C$) until shipment on dry ice to Great Lakes Institute for Environmental Research (GLIER) at the University of Windsor in Windsor, Ontario, Canada, for PCB and OC analyses. An aliquot of each egg homogenate (prepared by GLIER) was shipped to the National Wildlife Research Centre (NWRC) located in Ottawa, Ontario, Canada for PBDE and selected herbicide and fungicide analysis. NWRC is a Science and Technology Branch of the Canadian Wildlife Service (Environment Canada) located on the Carleton University campus. When applicable, gross deformities of embryos from failed eggs were examined by visual inspection (Gilbertson and others, 1991; Ludwig and others, 1993; Larson and others, 1996; Powell and others, 1996; Summer and others, 1996; Hoffman and others, 1998b; Kuiken and others, 1999; Fernie and others, 2003).

The osprey eggs were analyzed for PCB congeners, Aroclors, OC pesticides, PBDE congeners (as well as brominated biphenyl 101 [BB101] and hexabromocyclododecane [HBCD]), herbicides, and a fungicide:

PCB Congeners:

31/28	87	146	178	206
42	97	149	179	sum of PCB congeners (ΣPCBs)
44	99	151	180	
49	101/90	153	182/187	
52	105	158	183	
60/56	110	170/190	194	
64	118	171/156	195	
66/95	128	172	200	
70/76	138	174	201	
74	141	177	203/196	

Aroclor 1254:1260 (Aroclor 5460)
Aroclor 1260

OC Pesticides:

1,2,4,5-tetrachlorobenzene (1,2,4,5-TCB)	dieldrin
1,2,3,4-tetrachlorobenzene (1,2,3,4-TCB)	alpha-hexachlorocyclohexane (αHCH)
pentachlorobenzene (QCB)	beta-HCH (βHCH)
hexachlorobenzene (HCB)	gamma-HCH (γHCH)
octachlorostyrene (OCS)	oxychlordane
1,1,1-trichloro-2,2-bis(*p*-chlorophenyl)ethane (DDT)	*trans*-chlordane
1,1-dichloro-2,2-bis(*p*-chlorophenyl)ethylene (DDE)	*cis*-chlordane
1,1-dichloro-2,2-bis(*p*-chlorophenyl)ethane (DDD)	*trans*-nonachlor
mirex	*cis*-nonachlor
heptachlor epoxide (HE)	

PBDE Congeners, Brominated Biphenyl 101, and Hexabromocyclododecane:

17	153
28	154/BB153
47	183
49	190
66	209
85	sum of PBDE congeners (ΣPBDEs)
99	brominated biphenyl 101 (BB101)
100	hexabromocyclododecane (HBCD)
138	

Herbicides:

atrazine	picloram
cyanazine	methomyl
simazine	carbaryl
trichlopyr	2,4-dichlorophenoxyacetic acid (2,4-D)
alachlor	4-2,4-dichlorophenoxy butyric acid (2,4-DB)
metolachlor	2,4,5 trichlorophenoxy acetic acid (2,4,5-T)
silvex	2-methyl-4-chlorophenoxyacetic acid (MCPA)
dacthal	

dimethyl tetrachloroterephthalate (DCPA or dacthal and the isomer dimethyl-TCP [Di-TCP])

Fungicide:

chlorothalonil

In addition to the aforementioned contaminants, eggs collected in 2002–03 were analyzed for polychlorinated dibenzo-*p*-dioxins (PCDDs) and polychlorinated dibenzofurans (PCDFs). Residue concentrations of these contaminants in eggs collected in 2002–03 were low and thus eggs collected in 2006–07 were not analyzed for PCDDs and PCDFs.

Polychlorinated dibenzo-*p*-dioxins (PCDDs):

2378-tetrachlorodibenzo-*p*-dioxin (2378-TCDD)

total tetrachlorodibenzo-*p*-dioxin (total-TCDD)

12378-pentachlorodibenzo-*p*-dioxin (12378-P5CDD)

total pentachlorodibenzo-*p*-dioxin (total-P5CDD)

123478-hexachlorodibenzo-*p*-dioxin (123478-H6CDD)

123678-hexachlorodibenzo-*p*-dioxin (123678-H6CDD)

123789-hexachlorodibenzo-*p*-dioxin (123789-H6CDD)

total hexachlorodibenzo-*p*-dioxin (total-H6CDD)

1234678-heptachlorodibenzo-*p*-dioxin (1234678-H7CDD)

total heptachlorodibenzo-*p*-dioxin (total-H7CDD)

octachlorodibenzo-*p*-dioxin (OCDD)

Polychlorinated dibenzofurans (PCDFs):

2378-tetrachlorodibenzofuran (2378-TCDF)

total tetrachlorodibenzofuran (total-TCDF)

12378-pentachlorodibenzofuran (12378-P5CDF)

23478-pentachlorodibenzofuran (23478-P5CDF)

total pentachlorodibenzofuran (total-P5CDF)

123478-hexachlorodibenzofuran (123478-H6CDF)

234678-hexachlorodibenzofuran (234678-H6CDF)

123678-hexachlorodibenzofuran (123678-H6CDF)

123789-hexachlorodibenzofuran (123789-H6CDF)

total hexachlorodibenzofuran (total H6CDF)

1234678-heptachlorodibenzofuran (1234678-H7CDF)

1234789-heptachlorodibenzofuran (1234789-H7CDF)

total heptachlorodibenzofuran (total H7CDF)

octachlorodibenzofuran (OCDF)

OC pesticides and PCB fractions were analyzed separately on an electron-capture gas chromatograph (EC-GC) and the peaks were confirmed using gas chromatography/mass spectrometry (GC/MS). Co-planar PCBs, PCDDs, and PCDFs were analyzed by GC/MS. Quantification was accomplished by comparing sample-peak area against standard-peak area of three standards supplied by the Canadian Wildlife Service. Methodology for extraction and cleanup was confirmed by running sample blanks, replicate samples, and certified reference samples provided by the Canadian Wildlife Service for OC pesticides and PCBs, and by running a [13C]-surrogate spike for each sample analyzed for co-planar PCBs, PCDDs, and PCDFs (GLIER, 1995). Quality assurance/quality control (QA/QC) met Environment Canada standards. Brominated compounds were determined by GC/MS (Electron Capture Negative Ionization [ECNI]). An Agilent gas chromatograph (GC) 6890 equipped with a 5973 quadrupole mass spectrometer (MS) detector was used. Brominated compounds were identified on the basis of their retention times on the DB-5 columns and relative authentic standards (total-α-HBCD, BB-101, and PBDEs [14 congeners]). The α-HBCD is essentially total-α-HBCD as β- and γ-HBCD thermally isomerize to α-HBCD at GC temperatures >160°C. Quantification was performed using an internal standard method based on the relative ECNI response factor (RRF) of the 79Br+81Br anions of BDE-30 and to that of authentic congener standards. Mean recovery (± 1 standard error) of the internal standard was 98±1% in 2006 and 82±4% in 2007 for BDE-30. Concentrations were recovery-corrected as an internal standard method of quantification was used to reduce heterogeneity within and between analyte classes. The analytical precision of quantitative determinations was tested by repeated injections of standard compounds. Method blank samples were analyzed with each batch of five samples. The method limit of quantification was generally about 0.01 µg/kg ww for OCs and PCBs, 0.005 µg/kg ww for PBDEs, 2.0 ng/kg ww for herbicides, 0.3 ng/kg ww for dacthal, and 8.0 ng/kg ww for chlorothalonil. Residue concentrations were corrected to an approximate fresh wet weight using egg volumes (Stickel and others, 1973).

Nestling Plasma and Feathers

Blood samples were collected from a randomly selected nestling (about 35–45 days of age) at individual osprey nests on the LDR and the reference site WR in 2006 (LDR, N = 4; WR, N = 6) and 2007 (LDR, N = 3; WR, N = 0) (fig. 1). Morphological measurements (mass, wing-chord, and length of the 8th primary feather, center rectrix, and tarsus) were collected from all nestlings present at nests where blood samples were collected and each nestling was banded with a USGS Bird Banding Laboratory anodized lock-on band.

Nestling age was based on evaluation of results from a combination of techniques:
- Measurement of wing chord and length of the 8th primary (Schaadt and Bird 1993), plumage development (photographic record of known age nestlings, see: *http://www.cumauriceriver.org/pages/ef-slide/slide-ef.html*),
- Extrapolation from estimated date of egg-laying and hatching (based on visual inspection of embryo development in eggs collected for residue analysis at each respective nest), and
- Calculating the number of days between the observed hatch date to the sampling date.

Qualitative statements regarding the physical condition (respiration, body, feathers, legs, talons, eyes, cere, bill oral cavity) of each nestling also were assessed and recorded to provide a subjective measure of the overall condition (health) of osprey nestlings in addition to evaluation of hematological and biochemical determinations. To reduce potential variability within several hematological and biochemical parameters known to be influenced by circadian rhythms (García-Rodríguez and others, 1987b; Dawson and Bortolotti, 1997), nestling blood collection was conducted in the morning hours (8:00 am – 12:00 pm). Blood samples (about 5 mL) were collected from nestlings by brachial venipuncture (23-ga needle) into a 4.5 mL lithium-heparinized bead monovette syringe following the procedure described by Henny and Meeker (1981), Henny and others (1981), and pursuant to USGS Patuxent Wildlife Research Center (PWRC) Technical Operating Procedure CTP-48 (Hudson River Natural Resource Trustees, 2004). Samples were capped, gently inverted several times for mixing with heparin beads, and stored on wet ice immediately following each collection. Upon returning to the laboratory, chilled blood samples were mixed thoroughly on an electric rocker for approximately 5 minutes, a subsample was drawn into a microcapillary tube for hematocrit determinations (ca. 50 uL), and a blood smear was made. Hematocrits were determined by centrifuging the subsample (Microspin 24 Vulcon Technologies, approximately $10,000 \times g$ for 5 minutes) and then determining the packed cell volume (%) using a Microhematocrit Capillary Tube Reader (Oxford Labware®, MO). The remainder of the blood was centrifuged (approximately $2,500 \times g$ for 10 minutes) (IEC International Clinical Centrifuge®) and the plasma aspirated into three 2.5-mL cryotubes for residue analysis and biochemical assays. Plasma samples were preserved in liquid nitrogen immediately following aliquot preparation and later stored at -80°C until shipped to laboratories on dry ice. Two field blanks were prepared with laboratory-grade organic free water and were subjected to the same sampling, handling, and equipment as blood samples.

In conjunction with blood sampling, two to three breast feathers were collected from the same randomly selected nestling for mercury analysis (2006: LDR, N = 4; WR, N = 6). Feathers were placed in sterile plastic tubes until later cleaned with a solvent and sheared to improve digestion. Approximately 0.5 g homogenized tissue sample was digested for approximately 3 hours at 70–80° C with 5 mL of a 70:30 mixture of concentrated nitric and sulfuric acids. After cooling, samples were diluted to 20 mL with a 10% (v/v) solution of 0.2 N bromine monochloride. Total Hg was analyzed in oxidized water samples by cold vapor atomic fluorescence spectrometry (CVAFS) according to method FGS-069 (Frontier Geosciences Inc., Seattle, Washington).

Plasma samples were analyzed for the same congener-specific PCBs and OC pesticides as analyzed in eggs (see above) by gas chromatography at GLIER (Windsor, ON, Canada) using methods of Lazar and others (1992) described in detail in GLIER (1995). PBDEs, herbicides and fungicides (GC/MS: same profile as analyzed in eggs, see above) were analyzed at NWRC. Mean recovery (± 1 standard error) of the internal standard BDE-30 was102±3% in 2006 and 90±7% in 2007. The method limit of quantification was generally about 0.01 µg/kg ww for OCs and PCBs, and 0.03 µg/kg ww for PBDEs (herbicides and fungicides were not quantifiable in osprey plasmas). Hematology and biochemical determinations were conducted at the University of Miami School of Medicine, Comparative Pathology Laboratory (UMCPL), according to their "Advanced Well Bird Exam."

Protein fractions were determined using protein electrophoresis (Beckman Paragon Electrophoresis System, SPEP II gels) whereby plasma is applied to an electrical field on a gel substrate and proteins migrate on the gel dependent on their chemical charge. After staining, the protein bands are enumerated by laser densitometry. Total plasma protein (TPP) was determined by non-temperature compensated refractometer. Bile acids and hormone thyroxine (T4) were determined using Radioimmunoassay (RIA) analysis. All other biochemical determinations were evaluated using an Ortho Vitros 250 Chemistry Analyzer and hematology was assessed via blood slide smears.

Hematology determinations included:

Red blood cells	White blood cells
hematocrit	total white blood cells (WBC)
	lymphocytes
	monocytes
	eosinophils
	basophils
	heterophils

Plasma biochemical determinations included:

glucose (GLU) 540nm/37C/5min	triglycerides (TRIG)
aspartate aminotransferase (AST) 670nm/37C/5min	blood urea nitrogen (BUN) 670nm/37C/5min
creatine phosphokinase (CPK) 670nm/37C/5min	creatinine (CREA) 670nm/37C/5min
lactate dehydrogenase (LDH) 340nm/37C/5min	blood urea nitrogen/creatinine ratio (BCR)
alanine aminotransferase (ALT) 340nm/37C/5min	carbon dioxide (CO_2) 340nm/37C/5min
amylase (AMYL) 540nm/37C/5min	total plasma protein (TPP)
lipase (LI) 540nm/37C/5min	prealbumin (preALB)
uric acid (UA) 670nm/37C/5min	albumin (ALB)
total bile acids (TBA)	alpha 1 globulin (α1G)
calcium (Ca) 680nm/37C/5min	alpha 2 globulin (α2G)
phosphorus (PHOS) 670nm/37C/5min	beta globulin (βG)
sodium (Na) 37C/2min direct potentiometry	gamma globulin (γG)
potassium (K) 37C/2min direct potentiometry	albumin/globulin ratio (AGR)
cholesterol (CHOL) 540nm/37C/5min	thyroxine (T4)
gamma-glutamyl transpeptidase (GGT) 400nm/37C/5min	

Plasma samples also were sent to Patuxent Wildlife Research Center (PWRC), Laurel, Maryland for analyses and included some of the same parameters measured at the University of Miami (AST, ALT, CPK [measured as CK], GGT, UA, BUN, GLU, CREA, CHOL, PHOS, TRIG, TPP, ALB, Ca) as well as other biochemical parameters (total glutathione peroxidase [T-GSHpx], selenium-dependent glutathione peroxidase [S-GSHpx], glutathione reductase [GSSGred], alkaline phosphatase [alk phos], lactate dehydrogenase-L [LDH-L], and butyrylcholinesterase [BCHE]) that are known to reflect organ damage and related physiological disturbances. Basic methods and assay conditions are described by Hoffman and Heinz (1998a).

Plasma enzyme activities and constituents were measured at PWRC with a centrifugal analyzer (Centrifichem 500, Baker Instruments, Allentown, PA, USA) using methods previously described for ALT, alk phos, AST, BCHE, and CK (Hoffman and others, 1985, 1987); T-GSHpx, S-GSHpx, and GSSGred were measured using micromethods on the centrifugal analyzer (Habig and others, 1974). PWRC determinations were used in statistical analyses and reporting when serum chemistries were evaluated at both laboratories because PWRC conducts much contaminant research using blood samples of raptors.

Fish Collections

Fish species were collected for contaminant analysis using bottom trawl, hook and line, or directly from the hatchery. Fish were measured and weighed, individually wrapped in aluminum foil (dull side of foil in contact with fish), and stored on ice during transport, and stored at -20° C until further processed. Composite samples of whole fish were prepared using a Corenco industrial brand grinder and homogenates were placed in chemically cleaned I-Chem jars and again stored at -20° C until shipped on dry ice to GLIER for organic contaminant analysis (OCs and PCBs) and to NWRC for PBDE analysis. Composite samples contained two to seven individuals (table 1).

Biomagnification Factors

Fish to bird egg biomagnification factors (BMFs) were calculated using residue concentrations in composites of fish and eggs collected for this study. Percent incidence (occurrence) was determined for each fish species that were identified by photographic images of prey delivery events taken at the LDR study nests in 2006–07. Prey fish length was estimated relative to the tail length (205mm) of male osprey (Macnamara, 1972; see earlier methods section, "Osprey Foraging and Nesting Observations"). Fish length/weight information was obtained from Windward (2005a, 2005b) (Pacific staghorn sculpin [*Leptocottus armatus*], shiner surfperch [*Cymatogaster aggregate*], English sole, pile perch [*Rhacochilus vacca*]), Jim West and Kurt Stick (written commun., 2008, Washington Department of Fish and Wildlife [WDFW]) (Pacific herring [*Clupea pallasi*]), Roger Tabor (written commun., 2007, USFWS) (bullheads [*Ictalurus spp.*] and yellow perch [*Perca flavescens*]), and from measurement of study collections (salmonids [*Salmonidae*] and peamouth). Overall fish occurrence in the diet was evaluated on a nest-by-nest basis and each nest was weighted equally (N = 8); because the nest at Cecil Moses Memorial Park (CMP) did not have sufficient pre-incubation forging data (N = 5), this nest site was not included in percent occurrence calculations. Regression analysis was used to predict mass based on mean length and frequency distributions and mean weights were used to convert percent occurrence to percent biomass. Contaminant data were not available for several fish species because individuals (bullheads, smelts [*Osmerus spp.*], and PS starry flounder [*Platichthys stellatus*]) were not collected, thus peamouth residue data were used as a surrogate for bullheads, age 2–3+ year salmonid residues were used for smelts, and LDR starry flounder residues were used for PS starry flounder. Unidentified fish and fish from UNK capture locations were assumed to be captured by osprey in the same relative proportions observed in the identified portions of the diet.

Statistical Analysis

Prey fish delivered to nests were grouped according to family level identification. Prey fish were grouped by size class and assigned a single number (size index) to represent ranges of TL measurements (TL [mm]: <151 = 127, 152–201 = 178, 202–252 = 229, 253–303 = 279, 304–354 = 330, >355 = 381) and thereby estimate fish mass for descriptive statistics. Linear (peamouth) and quadratic (all other species) regression analysis was used to estimate fish mass based on length. Percent occurrence was determined for each fish family on an equally weighted nest-by-nest basis and mean mass was used to convert frequencies in diet to percent biomass (tables 2a and 2b). CMP did not have sufficient pre-incubation forging data (N = 5) and thus this nest site was not included in percent occurrence and biomass calculations for the pre-incubation period.

Contaminant concentrations were log-transformed for statistical analyses and presented as geometric means. The lower quantification limit was halved for samples in which a contaminant was not detected. This value was used to calculate geometric means when >50% of the samples contained detectable residues; means were not calculated when <50% of samples contained detectable residues. Because of unequal sample sizes, the General Linear Models (GLM) Procedure (Zar, 1999; SAS Institute, 2003) was used for analysis of variance and Tukey's Standardized Range Test (P < 0.05) was used to evaluate mean values when more than two groups were compared. A two-tailed Wilcoxon Rank Sum test was used to compare clutch size between LDR and WR nests (Zar, 1999). We combined LDR 2006 and 2007 egg and plasma samples because of small sample size, as contaminant concentrations were not significantly different between the two years for all but four PCB congeners (PCB 110, 118, 128) and four PBDE congeners (BDE 17, 28, 47, 66), which were all lower in 2006 compared to 2007. We converted contents of eggs to an approximately fresh wet weight (ww) using egg volume (Stickel and others, 1973); all egg residues are reported as fresh ww. Congener profiles were only visually compared. Toxic equivalent concentrations (TEQs) were calculated using 2002–03 data following Van den Berg and others (1998):

$$TEQ = \Sigma n1[PCDDi \times TEFi] + \Sigma n2[PCDFi \times TEFi] + \Sigma n3[PCBi \times TEFi]$$

where TEF is the toxic equivalency factor for birds. TEQs were not calculated using 2006–07 data because PCDDs and PCDFs were not analyzed in eggs, non-*ortho* PCBs were less than detection limits to be quantified, and mono-*ortho* PCBs in 2002–03 samples represented only 1–3% of the total TEQs, thus TEQs based only on mono-*ortho* PCBs would have little utility.

Hematological and biochemical parameters with non-normal distributions were log-transformed for descriptive statistics, GLM procedures, and correlations. We assessed relationships between contaminant concentrations and hematological/biochemical parameters in osprey nestling blood plasma using Pearson's correlation coefficients. Correlations were assessed when >50% of the samples contained detectable contaminant residues and the lower quantification limit was halved for samples in which a contaminant was not detected. To eliminate potential biases associated with age estimates derived by the techniques described in the methods section, "Tissue Sampling: Nestling Plasma and Feathers," wing chord and 8th primary measurements were used as an estimate of age (Schaadt and Bird, 1993) for evaluating relationships between age and blood plasma determinations because several of these parameters are known to be influenced by age (Campbell, 1995; Sturkie, 2000).

14

Results

Osprey Dietary Habits, Nesting Chronology and Productivity

The osprey diet in 2006–07 on the LDR was predominantly characterized by age 1 year hatchery-produced salmonids (primarily *Oncorhynchus* released into the LDR in late April) (61.0% [57.1% biomass], N = 213) during the pre-egg laying (pre-incubation) period (potential contaminant input into eggs) (tables 2a and 2b; fig. 2). Later, righteyed flounder (REF) (*Pleuronectidae*) (primarily soles), carps and minnows (CM) (*Cyprinidae*) (primarily peamouth), and salmonids (age 2–3+ year) were important during the nestling period (30.5%, 21.5%, 18.0% [28.0%, 19.3%, 34.4% biomass], respectively, N = 249). Because peamouth characterized the carp and minnow family (98.6%, N = 72) and soles predominately comprised the righteye flounder family (83.3%, N = 108) during the entire nesting period (2006: April 4–August 21, 2007: April 2–August 9), hereafter, REF will be referred to as soles and CM as peamouth (fig. 3). During the pre-egg laying period, 66.6% of the prey fish were captured in the LDR, while during the nestling period prey fish captured by osprey were more often from the PS (34.9%) and LW (28.7%) (N = 249) (fig. 4). As noted above, salmonids captured during the pre-egg laying period were predominantly captured in the LDR (91.1%) with the remaining 8.9% captured in the PS (includes EB, see section, "Methods") (excluding unknown capture locations) (N = 97) (fig. 5), and mostly consisted of recently released hatchery chinook (age 1 year) as indicated by mean length and weight (213 mm, 89 g). During the nestling period, salmonids were captured more frequently in the PS (59.6%) compared to the LDR (40.4%) and were notably larger fish (302 mm, 241 g) (table 2a), most likely representing immature resident chinook (age 2–3+ year). With respect to soles captured only during the nestling period (not including UNK capture locations), 90.6% were captured in the PS (N = 53); 98.6% of peamouth were captured in LW (entire nesting period, N=71; 100% during the nestling period N = 52). The diet of ospreys nesting along the WR is predominantly largescale suckers as reported by Henny and others (2003) (68.6 % [82.8 % biomass]), and Johnson and others (2008) (76.0% [92.7% biomass]).

Egg laying was initiated earlier on the WR than the LDR in 2006 (mean Julian date: 115 [April 24, 2006] and 138 [May 18, 2006], respectively; P < 0.0001) (table 3). Clutch initiation dates were based on back-calculation from observed estimates of embryo development days in the sample eggs collected for contaminant analysis based on a 38-day incubation period. Mean clutch size was significantly larger in WR (2006) nests than LDR (2006–07) nests (3.2 versus 2.3, Z = 1.9921, P = 0.0464). In 2006, 56% of nine active LDR nests were successful with two young produced from each of the five successful nests (table 4, fig. 1). The four nests near the mouth of the Duwamish Waterway all failed (two nests did not contain eggs on the planned day of egg collection, even though incubation posture was repeatedly observed several days prior to and following nest inspection). The number of young produced per active nest on the LDR in 2006 (at nests with egg and without egg collected) was 1.11, which is higher than the 0.80 young/active nest generally recognized necessary to maintain a stable population (Spitzer, 1980; Spitzer and others, 1983) (table 4). In 2007, 78% of nine LDR nests were successful. Two nests near the mouth of the Duwamish River that failed in 2006 failed again in 2007. Productivity based on young produced per active nest on the LDR in 2007 was 1.67. Nine of 10 WR active nests were successful in 2006 and 15 young were produced. In 2007 (no eggs were collected from WR nests), all 10 active nests were successful, producing 22 young. Thus, WR productivity was 1.50 in 2006 and 2.20 in 2007. The collection of a sample egg from a nest usually results in a reduction of 0.20–0.28 young per nest (Henny and others, 2008). Productivity on the LDR in 2003 was 1.42 for occupied nests and 1.55 for active nests (table 4).

Contaminant Residues in Osprey Eggs

2002–03 Results

Generally, osprey eggs collected adjacent to LW (N=3) during 2002–03 had the highest concentrations of ΣPCBs, coplanar PCBs, dioxins and furans, ΣPBDEs, and some of the OCs, (although none were significantly different from LDR eggs [N=7] except PCB 81) while SRE eggs (N=16) generally contained the lowest concentrations (table 5). Concentrations of PCDDs, PCDFs and coplanar PCBs in eggs from all locations generally were low. TEQs were highest for LW and lowest for SRE (231 and 43 ng/kg ww TCDD-equivalent) (table 5). Compared to SRE and LW eggs, LDR osprey eggs had the highest DDT, DDE, DDD, total chlordanes (not significantly different than LW eggs, but significantly different than SRE eggs), βHCH, and total Hg residues (not significantly different among groups). Mean concentrations of ΣPCBs in LW (2633 µg/kg ww) and LDR (1914 µg/kg ww) eggs (not significantly different, $\alpha = 0.05$) were higher and significantly different than eggs collected from SRE (742) (P <0.0001). PCB congener profiles were similar in osprey eggs collected from all sampling locations (fig. 6). Total Hg concentrations were not significantly different among the sampling locations (P = 0.5968) (table 5). The detected herbicide dacthal and an isomer of an unknown source (Di-TCP) were highest in SRE eggs (table 5); see Chu and others (2007) for additional data summary.

2006–07 Results

ΣPCBs were significantly higher in osprey eggs from the LDR than the WR (geometric means: LDR = 897.02 versus WR = 181.94 µg/kg ww, P = < 0.0001), and all but two congeners (PCB 64 and 172) followed the same pattern (both higher but not significantly different in the LDR) (table 6, figs. 7 and 8). OCs generally were higher, often significantly, in LDR eggs compared to WR eggs; exceptions to this pattern were DDE and dieldrin, which were not significantly different (geometric means LDR/WR µg/kg ww: 142.99/210.47, P = 0.6227 and 0.97/1.68, P = 0.1590, respectively) (table 7). Despite generally higher PCB and OC residue concentrations in LDR eggs compared to WR eggs, LDR egg residues are less than known effect level concentrations (ΣPCBs >25 mg/kg ww: Wiemeyer and others, 1988; Poole, 1989; Elliott and others, 2001; Martin and others, 2003; DDE > 4.2 mg/kg ww: Wiemeyer and others, 1988; HE > 1.5 mg/kg ww [mean concentration observed in American kestrel (*Falco sparverius*) eggs when productivity was reduced]: Henny and others, 1983; all other OC egg residue concentrations were lower than reported in previous studies when osprey productivity was not effected, see section, "Discussion"). Egg residues for all analyzed OCs and PCB congeners have decreased (most often significantly) since 2003 (most notably, geometric means 2003 and 2006–07: DDD 141.88 and 24.43 µg/kg ww, P = 0.0003; DDE 1197.33 and 142.99 µg/kg ww, P = 0.0169; ΣPCBs 1913.92 and 897.02 µg/kg ww, P = 0.0157) (tables 8 and 9). PBDE concentrations in 2003 and 2006–07 osprey eggs were not significantly different although trending upward (geometric means ΣPBDEs LDR 2003 and 2006–07: 213.82 and 298.51 µg/kg ww, P = 0.1992) (table 10). PBDE residues were higher in WR eggs (2006) than LDR eggs (2006–07) (geometric means ΣPBDEs LDR and WR: 320.89 and 897.44 µg/kg ww, P = 0.0003) (table 12, fig. 9). Di-TCP was significantly higher in WR than LDR eggs (P = 0.0477) (table 12). Dacthal was detected in one-half of the WR eggs (geometric mean 1.27 ng/kg ww) but in only 27% (3) of LDR eggs. Dacthal, Di-TCP, and chlorothalonil were not detected in LDR eggs collected in 2007. All other analyzed herbicides and fungicides were not detected in 2006–07. Total Hg concentrations in LDR eggs were lower in 2007 eggs compared to 2003 eggs (LDR eggs in 2006 were not analyzed for Hg) (P = 0.0453) (table 11). All contracted laboratories reported no analytical difficulties and all quality-control analyses were within acceptable limits.

Morphological, Hematological and Biochemical Osprey Nestling Measurements

Morphological measurements did not differ significantly between osprey nestlings sampled on the LDR (N=12, 2006–07) and WR (N=9, 2006) (table 13). In general, osprey nestlings were older and larger, but not significantly, on the WR compared to those on the LDR (mean age [days] LDR = 40.8 and WR = 44.4 [P = 0.21], mean mass [grams] LDR = 1,527 and WR = 1,632 [P = 0.26], mean wing chord [mm] LDR = 335 and WR = 349 [P = 0.42], mean primary [mm] LDR = 212 and WR = 221 [P = 0.59], and mean rectix [mm] LDR = 136 and WR = 136 [P = 0.99]. Hematocrit did not appear to be a function of time of day as there was no relationship between hour sampled and hematocrit (N = 13, P = 0.1689). Several hematological (hematocrit, heterophils, eosinophils) and biochemical (T-GSHpx, S-GSHpx, GLU, K, UA, AST, preALB, AGR, βG, γG, and TPP) determinations were significantly different between LDR and WR nestlings (table 14). Red and white blood cells and thrombin morphology was normal for all nestlings except one on the WR with toxic heterophils. Blood parasites were not detected in any of the prepared blood smears for individual nestlings.

Contaminant Residues in Osprey Nestling Plasma and Mercury in Feathers

PCB residues in nestling plasma (in 2006–07 in LDR and 2006 in WR) followed a similar pattern to that observed in eggs and were higher, most often significantly, in plasma from nestlings on the LDR compared to WR (geometric means ΣPCBs: LDR = 39.98 µg/kg ww, WR = 6.85 µg/kg ww, P = <0.0001) (table 15, figs. 7 and 8). Plasma concentrations of ΣPCB were 22–26 times lower than concentrations observed in eggs. PCB congeners 31/28, 44, 64, 70/76, 105, 141, 158, and 200 were only detected in 2007 LDR samples. OC plasma concentrations were not significantly different among the two rivers (except *cis*-nonachlor significantly higher in LDR nestlings, P = 0.0325) (table 16). One nestling on the LDR (CMP in 2007) and two nestlings on the WR (15B and 21 in 2006) contained relatively high DDE plasma concentrations (20.66, 53.65, and 20.59 µg/kg ww, respectively). ΣPBDEs (LDR/WR: 6.24/22.14 µg/kg ww) and congeners 47 (LDR/WR: 3.95/18.39 µg/kg ww) and 100 (LDR/WR: 0.80/1.99 µg/kg ww) were higher in WR plasmas compared to LDR plasmas (P = 0.0030, 0.0009, and 0.0424, respectively) (table 17, fig. 9). ΣPBDE plasma concentrations were 41–54 times lower than that observed in eggs (fig. 7), and while congeners 28, 49, 66, BB101, and 183 were not detected in all LDR and WR samples, congeners 17, 85, 138, 190, and 209 were not detected in any samples (table 17). As expected, lower contaminant concentrations generally were observed in nestling plasma compared to osprey eggs; however, a higher geometric mean concentration of dieldrin was observed in WR nestling plasma compared to the observed egg concentration. Herbicides and fungicides were not detected in any of the LDR or WR nestling plasma samples, and total Hg was not significantly different in feathers from nestlings on the two rivers (2006 LDR/WR: 2.19/2.32 mg/kg dry weight [dw], P = 0.8772) (table 17). All contracted laboratories reported no analytical difficulties and all quality-control analyses were within acceptable limits.

Congener profiles observed in osprey eggs and blood plasma varied slightly between rivers as well as between tissues (fig. 12). With respect to PCBs, congener 153 was the dominant congener observed in LDR and WR eggs followed by congener 138, while the opposite was observed in plasma (congener 138 was dominant followed by 153). In eggs, congener 180 was the third dominant congener as well as in LDR plasma, but congener 101/90 was the third most important component in WR plasma. LDR nestling plasma had a greater contribution of the lower chlorinated congeners compared to LDR eggs.

17

Correlations

PCB congeners 99, 183, 180, 138, 153, and ΣPCBs, as well as PBDE congeners 154/BB153, 153, 47, 100, 99 and ΣPBDE concentrations were significantly correlated between osprey eggs and nestling plasma ($P < 0.05$). Several blood plasma parameters and contaminant groups were significantly correlated (table 18). Total Hg concentrations were significantly correlated with calcium. As expected, estimated age was significantly correlated with wing chord ($R = 0.68$, $P = 0.0208$, $N = 11$) and length of the 8th primary ($R = 0.82$, $P = 0.0021$, $N = 11$), which indicated that age, estimated by calculating days between the observed hatch date and the sampling date, and age based on wing chord and 8th primary feather measurements (Schaadt and Bird, 1993) were similar and useful. Wing chord was not correlated with any contaminant group and length of the 8th primary was negatively correlated with one PCB congener (PCB 66/95). In several cases, the observed associations between blood plasma parameters and the major contaminant groups identified in osprey tissues (PCBs and PBDEs) followed opposite trends (for example: PCB congeners [including ΣPCBs in some cases] were positively associated with hematocrit, eosinophils, T-GSHpx, and S-GSHpx while PBDE congeners, including ΣPBDEs, were negatively associated with the same parameters. Likewise, heterophils and βG were negatively associated with PCB congeners and ΣPCBs while PBDE congeners and ΣPBDEs were positively associated with the same parameters) (table 18). Several PCB congeners were significantly associated with cellular parameters when no relationship was observed with ΣPCBs (most notably hematocrit and eosinophils, but also including PreALB, AST, URIC, and K). γG and TPP were positively associated with almost all PCB congeners and ΣPCBs but were not associated with any PBDE congeners or ΣPBDEs. T4 was negatively associated with DDE only. As expected, several blood plasma parameters were co-correlated.

Contaminant Residues in Fish

ΣPCBs were highest in shiner perch from the LDR (851.57 µg/kg, ww) followed by LDR English sole, LDR pacific staghorn sculpin, and LDR pile perch (636.69, 359.97, and 350.44 µg/kg ww, respectively) and lowest in yearling (age 1 year) salmonids collected from Soos Creek Hatchery (14.99 µg/kg ww) just prior to their late April release into the Green/Duwamish River (table 19, fig. 10). ΣPBDEs were highest in LW peamouth (51.0 µg/kg ww) and lowest in hatchery (age 1 year) salmonids (1.89 µg/kg ww) and LDR starry flounder (2.9 µg/kg ww). LW peamouth also contained the highest concentrations of DDE (120.74 µg/kg ww), DDD (35.33 µg/kg ww), total chlordane (72.46 µg/kg ww), HE (2.34 µg/kg ww), HBCD (1.4 µg/kg ww), among others (table 19, fig. 10). PCB congener patterns were similar for LDR fish and LW peamouth with congeners 153, 138, and 180 detected in the greatest proportions (fig. 11). Hatchery salmonids (age 1 year) and PS salmonids (age 2–3+ year) had similar PCB congener profiles, although PCB 74, followed by congeners 153, 138, and 149, respectively, were highest in LDR hatchery salmonids, while the highest congeners observed in the PS salmonids were 153, 138, and 149, respectively. PS fish (English sole and pacific staghorn sculpin) had similar PCB congener patterns with PCB 74 having the greatest ΣPCB contribution. PBDE 47 was detected in the greatest proportion for all fish species followed by congener 100 (table 19). Congener 99 was detected in high proportions in LDR English sole, hatchery salmonids, and PS salmonids. Generally, PCB and PBDE congener contributions in osprey eggs ($N = 11$) and in nestling plasma ($N = 7$) were similar to congener contributions observed in fish species (relative percent biomass proportions observed in the osprey diet, respective to each nesting period), although subtle differences were observed (fig. 13). Most notably, higher contributions of the lower chlorinated PCB congeners were observed in the fish diet (proportions relative to the pre-egg laying period) compared to LDR osprey eggs, and congener 101/90 was found in a greater contribution in fish species (proportions relative to the nestling period) compared to LDR plasma. Total Hg was highest in LDR shiner perch (0.56 mg/kg dw) and LW peamouth (0.54 mg/kg dw), and was lowest in hatchery salmonids (age 1 year) (0.09 mg/kg dw) (table 19). Chlorothalonil, dacthal, and Di-TCP were not detected in any fish samples.

Biomagnification Factors

Preliminary biomagnification factors (BMFs, fish to osprey eggs) were calculated on a wet weight basis and ranged from 0.1 to 15.4 for PCB congeners (ΣPCBs = 7.6), 0.3 to 94.3 for PBDE congeners (ΣPBDEs = 25.9), and 0.9 to 16.2 for OCs (table 20). Fish collections were limited and composite samples contained few individuals (7–10) (table 1). Due to sampling constraints associated with endangered fish species collections, only two individual age 2–3+ year chinook (inadvertently captured during hook/line sampling of other PS fish) comprised the composite sample, which is not an adequate sampling size to represent average contaminant residues for this age class of salmonids. Furthermore, no fish collections were made for smelts (within the 'other' category), bullheads, and starry flounder from the PS. Surrogate fish residue data (based on habits and habitats) were used for BMF calculations but inherently introduced variability. Ospreys nesting along the LDR primarily forage in the LDR, PS including EB, and LW. The foraging location for a small proportion of the observations was not determined (observer arrived at nest site and bird(s) was eating or the bird flew out of view and the capture could not be visually observed). In most cases, a capture location could be assumed based on the bird's departing and return flight path. Unidentified fish (osprey returned with partially consumed fish, which was unidentifiable, photograph image too distant for family level identification, and/or poor image quality) comprised 12.2% incidence of ospreys' diet during the pre-incubation period. Unidentified fish were assumed to be found in the same proportions of identified fish for BMF calculations. Because of the numerous postulations necessary to calculate BMFs, the limited number of composite samples (and in some cases numbers of individual fish comprising the composite: e.g., age 2–3+ year salmonids), and the lack of residue data for some species of fish, BMFs based on the data collected are weak estimates and not scientifically defensible.

Discussion

Osprey Dietary Habits, Nesting Chronology and Productivity

LDR ospreys predominately fed on hatchery-released salmonids primarily captured in the LDR during the pre-incubation period and soles (captured from PS), peamouth (captured from LW), and salmonids (age 2–3+ year) (captured most often from the PS) during the nestling period while WR ospreys ate predominantly largescale suckers throughout the nesting period (Henny and others, 2003; Johnson and others, 2008). The osprey population nesting along the WR numbered approximately 13 pairs in 1976 and increased to 234 pairs in 2001 (Henny and others, 2009a) and was much more established than the LDR population with only 7 pairs in 2003. As populations increase, new breeders from the denser population, often not producing full clutches or any clutch (Poole, 1989), disperse to other areas. More new and young breeders is one plausible explanation for why clutch size was smaller at LDR nests compared to WR nests, although many factors may influence clutch size (Poole and others, 2002). LDR birds began nesting later than WR birds and it is unknown whether this was a result of latitudinal differences (WR nests 44–45° N, LDR nests 47° N), less experienced breeders (younger birds nest later: Newton, 1979), or perhaps exposure to contaminants. A study with American kestrels reported *in ovo* PCB exposure suppresses egg laying, causes a delay in clutch initiation, and reduces clutch sizes and fledging success (Fernie and others, 2001a, 2001b). Although all analyzed PCB congeners in LDR eggs were less than suggested embryotoxic effect concentrations for raptors (ΣPCBs >25 mg/kg ww [equal to 25,000 µg/kg, the units reported in this document]: Wiemeyer and others, 1988; Poole, 1989; Elliott and others, 2001; Martin and others, 2003), historical information regarding the ability of ospreys to produce at these sites is not available. Despite relatively low contaminant residues in eggs, four nests at the mouth of the LDR failed in 2006 (T5, T18, T104, and T105) and two of those nests again failed in 2007 (T5 and T105). Furthermore, females at two of the failed nests in 2006 (T5 and T105) were repeatedly observed in the incubation posture prior to and after the egg collection date, although no egg(s) were present when the nest was visited for egg collection. Altered nesting behaviors have been associated with contaminant burdens (Peakall and Peakall, 1973; Tori and Peterle, 1983; Arena and others, 1999; McCarty and Secord, 1999a, 1999b; Fernie and others, 2001a), although egg residue concentrations (for the contaminants analyzed in this study) were less than recognized effect level concentrations and were not correlated with productivity (except for Di-TCP: R = -0.53, P = 0.0292, N = 17). Plausible explanations for LDR nest failure are:

- poorly conditioned individuals,
- inexperienced breeders, which tend to be less successful than older experienced breeders (Newton, 1979) (although we do not have data to support this hypothesis as adults were not aged and historical biological information is not known),
- embryo death from exposure to weather due to inconsistent incubation behaviors attributable to disturbance from humans/machinery, intruders (other ospreys), bald eagles (*Haliaeetus leucocephalus*), contaminant-related altered behavior, or other factors,
- limited prey abundance/availability/provisioning during critical time period with respect to individual adult female requirements for producing viable eggs,
- other contaminants not analyzed in this study,
- exposure to contaminants *in ovo,* which may be effecting adult reproductive potential (Fernie and others, 2001a, 2001b),
- additive or synergistic relationships among contaminants, or
- some combination of the aforementioned.

Contaminant Residues in Osprey Tissues

PCBs were significantly higher in osprey eggs and blood from the LDR than the WR, although were lower than that expected as Duwamish River fish are known to contain high PCB residues (Windward, 2004, 2006). If ospreys predominantly ate resident fish from the LDR during the pre-incubation period rather than hatchery-reared salmonids, residue concentrations in eggs would have been much higher as LDR fish contain higher concentrations than hatchery salmonids and fish from adjacent areas (table 19; Windward, 2005a, 2005b). Other fish-eating avian species observed in the LDR (such as pigeon guillemots [*Cepphus columba*] and common mergansers [*Mergus merganser*]) are not necessarily better sentinel species for monitoring contaminants in the LDR because:

- they also are likely eating hatchery-reared salmonids,
- are likely feeding in other PS areas,
- are not known to consume the larger fish (pigeon guillemots typically feed on fish 60-150 mm: Ewins, 1993) found in the LDR (starry flounder, pile perch, English sole, Pacific staghorn sculpin) or prefer salmonids over non-salmonids and generally forage on the most abundant, suitably sized prey (mergansers: citations within Mallory and Metz, 1999), and
- do not solely feed on fish (Ewins, 1993; Mallory and Metz, 1999).

20

Although guillemots and mergansers may feed on LDR shiner perch, these fish are not readily available during the pre-egg laying nesting period (Jim Shannon, Senior Scientist, David Evans and Associates Inc., oral commun., 2007). Furthermore, guillemots infrequently use the LDR and mergansers do not nest along the LDR (Windward, 2003). Thus, these avian species have no biomonitoring advantages and are not better sentinels than osprey to use for monitoring contaminants in the LDR. Moreover, other fish-eating birds observed in variable frequencies and numbers in the LDR (great blue herons, gull spp. [*Larus spp.*], bald eagles, tern spp. [*Sterna spp.*], belted kingfishers [*Megaceryle alcyon*], and grebe spp. [*Podiceps, Podilymbus, and Aechmophorus spp.*]) are not considered more suitable for LDR contaminant monitoring than osprey for the same reasons mentioned.

Mean ΣPCB residues in LDR eggs have decreased by 53% since 2003 and were slightly higher than mean ΣPCB residues reported for osprey nesting along the Columbia River, WA and OR in 2004 (Henny and others, 2008). ΣPCB residues in 2006–07 LDR eggs (897 µg/kg ww [equal to 0.9 mg/kg ww]) were lower than ΣPCB residues reported in osprey eggs collected from the Canadian Great Lakes Basin during 1991–1995 (7.1 mg/kg) when productivity was not effected by contaminants (Martin and others, 2003), lower than the concentration associated with embryotoxic effects (ΣPCBs >25 mg/kg ww [equal to 25,000 µg/kg, the units reported in this document]: Wiemeyer and others, 1988; Poole, 1989; Elliott and others, 2001), and lower than concentrations (in eggs: 5–10 mg/kg ww [equal to 5,000–10,000 µg/kg]) associated with healthy productivity (one young per active nesting pair of adults) for eagles (Hoffman and others, 1996b). ΣPCB residues in LDR nestling blood were identical (40 µg/kg) to ΣPCB residues reported for bald eagle nestlings sampled in 2003 from Nanaimo-Crofton, Vancouver, British Columbia (BC) and higher than other sites sampled in southwestern BC (McKinney and others, 2006). ΣPCB residues in LDR osprey nestling plasma were lower than ΣPCB residues reported for osprey nestling plasma sampled from 1991 to 1995 in the Great Lakes (Martin and others, 2003) when productivity exceeded the threshold (0.8 young) regarded necessary to maintain a stable population. In contrast, much higher mean ΣPCB and DDE levels in bald eagle nestling plasma from Lake Superior (127 and 25 µg/kg ww) and Lake Erie (199 and 22 µg/kg ww) were suggested to be adversely affecting reproduction because nests with chicks containing the highest concentrations of PCBs and DDE were shown to have the lowest productivity (Bowerman and others, 1993, 1995). These previously reported concentrations described above are higher than mean residues observed in LDR and WR osprey eggs and nestling plasma. While one nestling from the LDR contained ΣPCB and DDE plasma residues (CMP 2007: 84 and 21 µg/kg ww) similar to the aforementioned concentrations correlated with impaired reproductive potential in bald eagles (ΣPCB: 47–199 and DDE: 20–35 µg/kg ww: Bowerman and others, 1993, 1995), this nest successfully fledged two osprey young in 2007. This nest also contained two addled eggs (one was analyzed) in 2007 but residues for all analyzed contaminants were less than known effect level concentrations. Additionally, two osprey nestlings on the WR (nests 15B and 21 in 2006) contained plasma DDE concentrations (53.65 and 20.59 µg/kg ww) comparable to concentrations associated with decreased productivity in bald eagles described above, but these nests also successfully fledged young (two and one young, respectively).

ΣPBDEs were significantly lower in osprey eggs and blood from the LDR than WR nestlings. Although effect levels for PBDEs are not precisely known, it has been suggested that concentrations greater than 1,000 µg/kg ww may reduce osprey reproductive performance (Henny and others, 2009b). Mean ΣPBDE concentrations found in WR osprey eggs (897 µg/kg ww) were unexpectedly some of the highest reported in literature (see Norstrom and others, 2002; Gauthier and others, 2008). Mean ΣPBDEs in WR nestling plasma (22 µg/kg) were higher than concentrations reported in bald eagle nestling plasma sampled in 2003 from southwestern BC, but lower than residues reported for Santa Catalina Island, California, in 2001 (31 µg/kg)

(McKinney and others, 2006). Mean ΣPBDEs in LDR osprey nestling blood were comparable to residues in bald eagle nestling plasma sampled from southwestern BC: slightly lower than residues in nestlings from Nanaimo-Crofton and higher than other sampled sites (McKinney and others, 2006). Other OC contaminants analyzed in osprey eggs and plasma were lower than concentrations previously reported for osprey in the Pacific Northwest when the respective sampled populations were increasing (Henny and others, 2003, 2004).

Differences in PCB congener profiles between LDR osprey eggs and nestling blood could not be explained by variation in diet alone because congener profiles in fish species (in biomass proportions observed in the diet during each respective nesting period) generally were similar (fig. 13). Differences in congener compositions between eggs and plasma may be attributed to differences in the ability of juvenile and adult osprey to metabolize PCBs. de Solla and Martin (2009) found weak evidence for this hypothesis in their study with ospreys exposed to local PCB sources. More specifically, similar to findings by de Solla and Martin (2009), osprey chick plasma generally had a higher proportion of PCBs that were metabolized by P450 2B (PCB groups II and IV; Kannan and others, 1995) compared to proportions observed in adult eggs for the same groups (fig. 14). Furthermore, adult eggs generally had higher proportions of PCBs not metabolizable (Group I) compared to chick plasma Group I proportions. While it is possible eggs represent a proportion of contaminant burdens acquired by adult osprey on their wintering ground as the half-lives for many organochlorines are more than 6 months in birds (Norstrom and others, 1986; Clark and others, 1987), ospreys generally are income breeders, acquiring lipid and protein from local sources (Drent and Daan, 1980) and Elliott and others (2007) found DDE burdens in osprey eggs were more related to their breeding grounds than their wintering grounds. Greater variation in PCB congener proportions observed between WR eggs and plasma may represent differences in food habits during the individual nesting periods (pre-egg laying and nestling period) as previous dietary studies on the WR evaluated the entire nesting period (Henny and others, 2003; Johnson and others, 2008) rather than individual periods.

Contaminant Residues in Fish

Contaminant residues observed in fish composites were lower than previously reported in literature (Windward, 2004; Johnson and others, 2007) suggesting that the LDR is getting cleaner with respect to legacy contaminants measured in this study (OCs, PCBs). Similar decreases in contaminant residues in LDR fish have been reported previously (Stein and others, 1995: ΣLPAHs, ΣHPAHs, ΣPCBs, ΣDDTs decreased from 1989 to 1990; Meador and others, 2002: mean ΣPCBs decreased from 1989 to 1993 and from 1993 to 2000 in Chinook salmon). However, residues were higher in fish and crab species in 2004 than during 1995–1998, 2005, and 2006 suggesting that contaminant exposure may be greatest immediately following dredging events (Windward, 2007b). While much of the sediment contamination in the LDR is thought to be partially buried by recently deposited sediment (the highest contaminant concentrations generally are detected 6 inches beneath the sediment surface, although high residues have been detected in surface sediment in localized hotspots [ECOSS, 2008]), buried contaminated sediments become available during and after dredging events, which occur regularly in the LDR. Although decreases in PCB residues in avian eggs have been noted in the Willamette and Columbia rivers (Henny and others, 2004; 2008; 2009a), and the Great Lakes (Hebert and others, 1994; Stow, 1995), in some areas PCB concentrations more recently have stabilized (gull eggs from the Great Lakes: Stow, 1995; bald eagle nestling plasma: Donaldson and others, 1999). In the current study, PCB concentrations were highest in LDR shiner surfperch, English sole, and pacific staghorn sculpin, respectively, the same pattern reported by Windward (2005a, 2005b). Furthermore, OC, PCB and PBDE concentrations were higher in age 2–3+ year salmonids than in age 1 year salmonids, although caution is required in data interpretation because few samples were available (N = 2, age 2–3+ year salmonids analyzed). A similar pattern was reported by Windward (2004) for salmonids collected in May; however, the opposite trend was observed for fish samples collected in June (ΣPCB residues were higher in hatchery salmonids than in wild salmonids). Meador and others (2002) also reported higher ΣPCBs in hatchery Chinook than in wild Chinook. McCain and others (1990) indicated salmonids bioaccumulate substantial levels of toxic chemicals during their residency in the Duwamish estuary; and residues observed in hatchery salmonids collected directly from the hatchery for this study would likely be higher following exposure to LDR contaminants. PBDE concentrations in LDR fish were lower than peamouth collected from LW, similar to spatial patterns observed by Johnson and others (2006) in which PBDE residues in largescale sucker fillets were lower in LDR than LW samples. Residue concentrations in fish (collected in this study and compared to concentrations reported in previous studies) and osprey eggs collected in multiple years of this study indicate an upward trend of PBDEs in the LDR, similar to observations in biota elsewhere (Norstrom and others, 2002; Rayne and others, 2003), including osprey eggs (Henny and others, 2009b).

Biomagnification Factors

BMFs for PCBs were slightly lower than previously reported by Henny and others (2004, 2009a). The BMFs for ΣPCBs calculated in this study were 7.6 compared to 11 and 8.4 reported by Henny and others (2004, 2009a). BMFs for OCs also were lower than previously reported, most notably for DDT, DDD and DDE (5.6, 3.3, 5.0, respectively compared to 47, 23, 87 [Henny and others, 2004] and not calculated, 18, 79 [Henny and others, 2009a], respectively). BMFs for PBDEs have not been previously reported and were higher than PCB BMFs using the dataset generated in this study. This dataset involved low contaminant residues in fish (especially hatchery-reared salmonids collected directly from the hatchery that were a high percentage of the diet during the pre-egg laying period) and in osprey eggs, small sample sizes for both eggs and fish, and a complicated feeding strategy, thus BMFs calculated with this dataset have limited usefulness (Henny and others, 2009a). Furthermore, it must be recognized that the diet of the LDR osprey population during the pre-egg laying period does not accurately represent existing contaminant burdens in resident LDR fish.

Hematological and Biochemical Osprey Nestling Measurements

The health status of raptor populations has traditionally been assessed using measures of population size, reproductive success and (or) survival. Although these measures provide valuable biological and ecological information, most often they do not aid biologists in identifying problems until after a significant effect (reduced productivity) has been observed on a large scale. As legacy contaminant residues decrease in many areas (Willamette and Columbia rivers: Henny and others, 2008, 2009a; Great Lakes: Hebert and others, 1994 and Stow, 1995), greater emphasis and interest is being placed on the effects of chronic, low-level contaminant exposure in addition to emerging contaminants. The utilization of hematological and serum chemistry has gained popularity as an additional method for assessing and monitoring the health of wild birds (Newman and others, 1997; Balbontin and Ferrer, 2002), and for potentially determining the effects of chronic, low-level, sub-lethal exposure to environmental toxicants, which has proven useful in the management of white-tailed deer (Redig and others, 1983). This study incorporates blood sampling from osprey nestlings to assess contaminant burdens and the associated physiological state of nestlings as an indicator of the stress induced by exposure to contaminants, which may be particularly relevant because the most sensitive stage for adverse effects by PCBs appears to be the prenatal and the early postnatal period (monkeys and rats; Brouwer and others, 1999). Generally, hematological and biochemical determinations are species specific and most of the existing data and established "reference ranges" has been derived primarily from captive psittacines (parrots, macaws), other domesticated fowl (poultry), or waterfowl and raptors maintained in zoos or aquariums (Smith and Bush, 1978; Halliwell, 1981; International Species Information System, 1983; Polo and others, 1992; Harr, 2002). More recent studies report data from free-living species in order to establish baseline data and reference ranges (Newman and others, 1997; Bowerman and others, 2000b; Lanzarot and others, 2001; Balbontin and Ferrer, 2002; Mealey and others, 2004); however, none of these studies incorporate osprey. Although many have assessed the influence of intrinsic and extrinsic factors on the variability of the blood parameters measured in this study (Okumura and Tasaki, 1969; Gee and others, 1981; Rehder and others, 1982; García-Rodríguez et and others, 1987a, 1987b), few have assessed the influence of contaminants on these same parameters.

Hematological and biochemical determinations provide valuable nutritional and physiological information that help assess the fitness of an individual (or population), which may have broader biological and ecological implications. Difficulty in ascertaining normal from abnormal cellular determinations is widely recognized because reference data are not available for most species, responses can be species specific, and values are known to fluctuate greatly within and between populations and to be influenced by several factors: age, sex, nutritional condition and diet, physiological state, circadian rhythm, environmental conditions, methodologies (storage and analytical methods including instruments and reagents used), and others (Okumura and Tasaki, 1969; Twiest and Smith, 1970; Gee and others, 1981; Chaplin and others, 1984; Ferrer and others, 1987; García-Rodríguez and others, 1987a, 1987b; Bustamante and Traviani, 1994; Hochleithner, 1999; Fair and others, 2007). Due to the aforementioned, the acknowledgement that no one parameter is specific of a particular disease or overall condition, and that individual parameters may respond to several factors in the same manner (Hochleithner, 1999), evaluating blood and plasma determinations collectively is imperative when assessing the health of an individual or a population. As long as limitations are taken into account when interpreting data, blood sampling can be a useful nondestructive tool for detecting reduced health of wild bird populations, which may have broader ecological implications.

Despite unavailable reference values, small sample size, and recognized limitations, significant statistical differences ($\alpha = 0.05$) in several hematological and biochemical measurements (hematocrit, heterophils, eosinophils, AST, T-GSHpx, S-GSHpx, GLU, K, UA, preALB, βG, γG, AGR, and TPP) were observed between osprey nestlings sampled from the LDR and WR. Although authors recognize that residue concentrations generally were low in osprey tissues, chronic low-level exposure effects are not well understood and are complicated by the fact that long-term studies with the same individuals are necessary for evaluating sub-lethal effects. Several major differences existed between the studied rivers (PCB and PBDE residue concentrations, food habits, habitats, etc.), which limited the ability to identify which characteristic(s) is most responsible for the observed hematological and biochemical differences. Further, because the small dataset did not allow for the use of multivariate statistics, a number of individual tests were conducted to evaluate parameter differences between rivers and to assess relationships between contaminants and biochemical parameters, consequently with a proportion of the results significant due to chance alone. Specifically, 41 individual tests were run to assess differences in bioindicators between LDR and WR nestlings and 1,444 correlations (38 chemicals with 38 bioindicators) were assessed at $\alpha = 0.05$, thus approximately 2 and 72, respectively, of the results may be significant due to chance, further identifying the need for caution with data interpretation. For the purpose of this study and the Elliott Bay Natural Resource Trustees' interest in the LDR, hematological and biochemical differences will be discussed with respect to potential injury to LDR osprey nestlings.

Differences in hematocrit, heterophils, and eosinophils are likely of little consequence to the health of LDR nestlings as determinations in LDR nestlings generally were within ranges reported for diurnal birds of prey (Mauro, 1987). LDR AST values (higher than WR determinations) were lower than reported for other free-living and captive young and adult avian species (Halliwell, 1981; Polo and others, 1992; Bowerman and others, 2000b; Balbontin and Ferrer, 2002; Mealey and others, 2004). AST is the most sensitive indicator of liver disease in pigeons; however, it is not liver specific as elevated concentrations also are observed in muscle disease (Lumeij, 1994). Fudge (1997) reported that AST values <50 U/L indicate end-stage liver disease and Lumeij (in Fudge, 1997) found that plasma from birds with advanced liver disease may have abnormally low AST concentrations. AST determinations are an indication of enzyme activity and not organ function (Hochleithner, 1999) and because AST reference values are not available for osprey, it is not known whether ospreys have 'normally' low AST concentrations compared to other raptor species. Interpretation is complicated by the fact that osprey tissues collected from the reference site selected for this study unexpectedly contained high PBDE concentrations limiting the utility of the reference data. AST concentrations were <50 U/L in all LDR and WR nestlings, and concentrations were negatively correlated with dieldrin, positively correlated with four PCB congeners (PCB 99, 128, 174, and 177), and negatively correlated with BDE-47 and ΣPBDEs (R = -0.63, 0.68, 0.59, 0.62, 0.59, -0.68, -0.64, respectively; P<0.05). AST concentrations may in fact be lower for ospreys than AST concentrations in other raptor species although further study is necessary. Residue concentrations in LDR plasmas for the analyzed contaminants were low, nestlings appeared in good condition at the time of sampling, and were observed to fledge age suggesting that LDR nestlings were likely not coping with end-stage liver disease.

T-GSHpx and S-GSHpx are metabolic enzymes and an indication of oxidative stress (Hoffman, 1998a). Oxidative stress can lead to cell death by triggering apoptosis and may cause necrosis. Although reference ranges are not available, increased GSH peroxidase levels protect cell proteins and cell membranes against oxidation (Meister, 1988). GSH peroxidases use GSH (glutathione: an antioxidant involved in the multiplication of lymphocytes and antibody response) to reduce H_2O_2 and organic peroxides and form GSSG. GSSG is then reduced to GSH via GSSGred and the pentose phosphate pathway and GSH is effectively recycled. Deficiencies in the antioxidant system make biological species more susceptible to toxic agents and potential toxicities (Cossu and others, 1997). T-GSHpx and S-GSHpx determinations were significantly higher in LDR nestlings than in WR nestlings and for the aforementioned reasons, LDR nestlings were deemed better suited to cope with oxidative stress compared to WR nestlings (D.J. Hoffman, Research Physiologist, PWRC, oral commun., 2008). Several OC and PCB contaminants (including ΣPCBs) were positively correlated with T-GSHpx and S-GSHpx while BDE-47 and ΣPBDEs were negatively associated with both enzymes. Freshwater bivalves exposed to contaminated sediments (from a complex industrial effluent of a cokery) for 8 days underwent rapid depletions of GSH and reductions of selenium dependent glutathione peroxidase and glutathione reductase activities (Doyotte and others, 1997). Fernie and others, (2005b) found that exposure to PBDEs resulted in hepatic oxidative stress and subsequent changes in glutathione metabolism in American kestrels. Raldúa and others (2008) found a positive relationship between T-GSHpx and ΣPBDEs in barbels (a species of fish in the *Cyprinidae* family found in Spain). Decreased GSH peroxidase enzyme activity was observed in mallards exposed to mercury (Hoffman and others, 1998a). Blom and Förlin (1997) found long-term exposure to PCBs induced glutathione transferase (an enzyme also involved in detoxification). Further study is warranted to better understand the differences of these metabolic enzymes and the biological significance of the values obtained in this study.

Differences between LDR and WR nestlings with respect to GLUC, URIC, and K were most likely attributed to dietary differences or differences in feeding frequencies (García-Rodríguez and others, 1987a; Totzke and others, 1999) because values for all nestlings were within the reference ranges reported in previous studies for raptorial species (Halliwell, 1981; Joseph, 1999) and within the reference ranges for captive psittacines provided by the contracting laboratory. Significant correlations did exist between several PCB congeners and GLUC, URIC, and K but these relationships did not exist when associations were evaluated with nestlings from each river separately (WR, N = 6 evaluated separately from LDR, N = 7). UA (higher in LDR than in WR nestlings) increases with dietary protein intake and K can fluctuate depending on the amount of K in the diet. Food habits were notably different between LDR and WR nestlings and because determinations were within ranges reported in previous studies, food habits are the most plausible reason for observed differences.

Many plasma proteins were significantly different between river nestlings (TPP, PreAlb, βG, γG, and AGR). Most plasma proteins are synthesized by the liver, except for the immunoglobulins (produced by lymphocytes and plasma cells). Plasma proteins function as contributors to oncotic pressure, transport substances (lipids, Ca, hemoglobin, iron), regulate inflammatory response, and provide resistance to infection by binding antigens in the form of immunoglobulins during disease (Jones, 1999; Thomas, 2000). The concentration of plasma proteins is a function of hormonal balance, nutritional status, water balance and other health factors (Jain, 1993). TPP (which includes albumin, preALB, globulins and fibrinogen; Jain, 1993) concentrations between 3.0–6.0 g/dL are considered normal for most avian species (Campbell and Dein, 1984), while Jones (1999) suggests 3.5–5.5 g/dL for raptors, and a value <2.5 g/dL is considered a grave prognosis (Campbell and Dein, 1984). TPP was significantly lower in nestlings from the LDR (2.8 g/dL) than the WR (3.5 g/dL), lower than concentrations considered "normal," and lower than means but within the 95% confidence limits (at the lower limits) reported for captive bald eagle adults (Tatum and others, 2000). Mean TPP in LDR nestlings were less than means, but within ranges reported for bald eagle nestlings by Bowerman and others (2000b) and Mealey and others (2004) although these studies were carried out in known contaminated areas (Great Lakes: Bowerman and others, 1995, 2000a and Florida Bay: Lounsbury-Billie and others, 2008; Perry, 2008). Bowerman and others (2000b) noted lymphocytes varied as a function of OC and PCB concentrations in blood plasma but that none of the other parameters were significantly different in eagles from the Great Lakes and lower contaminated inland breeding areas (Bowerman, 1993; Bowerman and others, 1995). Contaminants, if evaluated, in eagle nestlings from Florida Bay were not presented in Mealey and others (2004). LDR TPP was within ranges reported for free-living Bonelli's eagle (*Hieraaetus fasciatus*) nestlings in Spain (Balbontín and Ferrer, 2002) and within reference ranges for captive psittacines provided by the contracting laboratory. Physiologic factors (age, gender, dietary protein, temperature stress, hydration state, hemorrhage or inflammation) may affect protein levels (Sturkie *in* Hochleithner, 1999), and while age was not statistically different among nestlings from the LDR and WR, diet was notably different. Leveille and Sauberlich (1961) found increases in dietary protein increases total protein and albumin; however, albumin was similar for LDR and WR nestlings (LDR = 1.42, WR = 1.41). Furthermore, Hochleithner (1999) indicated that the effect of diet on TPP is subtle and difficult to interpret. Negative relationships were observed between TPP and several PCB congeners, ΣPCBs, and *cis*-nonachlor suggesting these contaminants may be influencing TPP, although further study is warranted. Using the data generated in this study, we were not able to determine which parameter, if any, was most responsible for the observed differences in TPP between LDR and WR nestlings, although globulins (βG and γG, components of TPP) were lower in LDR nestlings and are likely one reason lower concentrations of TPP were observed in LDR nestlings.

26

γG (primarily composed of immunoglobulins) were lower in LDR nestlings than WR nestlings and lower than reported for birds of prey (Halliwell, 1981). In fact, mean γG in LDR nestlings was lower than the range observed in WR nestlings. The mean LDR γG was lower than means reported for peregrine falcon (*Falco peregrinus*) nestlings (Lanzarot and others, 2001) but within the 95% confidence limits (although the lowest limit reported), lower than means but within the 95% confidence limits (at the lower limits) reported for captive bald eagle adults (Tatum and others, 2000), and within reference ranges for captive psittacines provided by the contracting laboratory. γG consist mostly of circulating antibodies produced by the lymphoid organs (Campbell and Dein, 1984); decreased concentrations are associated with acquired or inherited immunodeficiency and failure of passive transport (Jain, 1993; Thomas, 2000). Previous studies assessing the effects of a contaminant group(s) on hematological and biochemical responses in raptors have shown that various contaminants cause immunosuppression (Grasman and others, 1996, 2000; Grasman and Fox, 2001; Fernie and others 2005a) rendering an avian host more vulnerable to certain types of infection (Friend and Trainer, 1970; Sagerup and others, 2000). Brouwer and others (1999) reported that exposure to PCBs, even at low exposures, particularly relevant during the early stages of life, causes immunotoxicity. Furthermore, Varanasi and others (1993) reported that immune competence of juvenile salmon from the Duwamish Waterway was suppressed and was most likely due to contaminants based on subsequent laboratory study. Casillas and others (1997) reported juvenile chinook salmon from a contaminated urban estuary, but not from a nonurban uncontaminated estuary, were more susceptible to a virulent marine bacterium than fish from the corresponding hatchery. All PCB congeners except for two (PCB 66/95 and 156/171) and ΣPCBs were negatively correlated with γG (ΣPCBs: $R = -0.73$, $P = 0.0042$), suggesting that PCBs may be playing a role in the lower γG concentrations in LDR nestling plasma compared to WR nestling plasma. A recent study by Laetz and others (2009) reported that mixtures of pesticides were additive and synergistic in the endangered Pacific salmon (*Oncorhynchus spp.*), that several combinations of organophosphates were lethal at concentrations that in single-chemical trials were sublethal, and that mixtures may be a more important to the species recovery than originally expected. If ospreys are immunosuppressed then contaminant concentrations lower than that known to cause effects would likely be of greater importance to the health and survival of ospreys. Furthermore, additive or synergistic relationships among contaminants would likely lower the concentration at which a contaminant(s) is toxic which may be particularly relevant if an organism is immunologically compromised. Osprey reference values for γG are not available and although it is possible LDR nestlings may be immunologically compromised, further investigation is warranted to determine if the globulin concentrations observed in LDR birds is biologically significant since nestlings were observed until fledge age (about 50 days) and their fate thereafter is unknown.

βG (acute phase proteins) also were lower in LDR nestlings than WR nestlings. Mean βG determinations for both river nestlings were within 95% confidence limits reported for peregrine falcon nestlings (Lanzarot and others, 2001) and captive bald eagle adults (Tatum and others, 2000), within reported reference ranges for raptors (Werner and Reavill, 1999), although higher than ranges reported by Halliwell (1981). In fact, βG for LDR nestlings were within reference ranges for captive psittacines provided by the contracting laboratory while WR nestling βGs were higher than ranges provided by the laboratory. Increases in βG are associated with inflammation (acute or chronic) (Thomas, 2000), infection (Campbell and Dein, 1984), active liver disease (Jain, 1993; Duncan and others, 1994; Thomas, 2000), nephrotic syndrome (Thomas, 2000), and malnutrition (Werner and Reavill, 1999). Decreases in βG are associated with hepatic insufficiency, severe inanition, blood loss and protein-losing states (Werner and Reavill, 1999). Correlations were observed between various PCB congeners including ΣPCBs (negative trends) as well as BDE47 and ΣPBDEs (positive trends). Because reference values are not available for osprey, identifying what factor(s) is most responsible for the observed βG differences in nestlings between rivers was not determined. Contrary to our findings, Grasman and others (2000) reported positive associations between PCBs and β2G in herring gulls (*Larus argentatus*) and between PCBs and β1G in Caspian terns (*Sterna caspia*). Although AGR was significantly higher in LDR nestlings than WR nestlings, all values were within ranges reported by Lanzarot and others (2001). Observed differences of nestlings between rivers were most likely due to differences observed in globulins because albumin was similar (LDR 1.42, WR 1.41).

The clinical significance of preALB (a transporter protein for thyroxine produced by the liver) is unknown and determinations were lower in LDR than WR nestlings. In humans, preALB decreases with malnutrition, surgery, trauma, and infections (Jain, 1993). Decreased concentrations may suggest decreased synthesis from impaired liver function and increased loss through the kidneys (Jain, 1993). PreALB has not been reported frequently in other avian studies although it has been observed to decrease with inflammation in other species (Jain, 1993). PreALB was lower in LDR nestlings than reported for peregrine falcon nestlings from Spain (Lanzarot, 2001), lower than means but within 95% confidence limits reported for bald eagles (Tatum and others, 2000), and lower than reference ranges for captive psittacines provided by the contracting laboratory. Negative associations were observed between PreALB and three PCB congeners (PCB 110, 146, and 180), and Aroclor 1260, and a positive association was observed with BDE 47. Further study is necessary to determine the major factor(s) most responsible for differences observed in nestlings between rivers.

Correlations

Many associations between contaminant groups and hematological/biochemical parameters were observed although the statistical associations observed do not necessarily imply causal relationships. We suggest using caution when interpreting associations because:

- sample size was low,
- some significant relationships observed when applying data from all nestlings (LDR and WR N = 13) were not observed when correlations were made with LDR nestlings (N = 7) or WR nestlings (N = 6),
- many contaminant groups (and congeners within) were co-correlated,
- various contaminant groups were correlated with the same hematological/biochemical parameter(s),
- other differences (food habits, habitats) existed between LDR and WR nestlings, and
- other factors and contaminants not measured could be influencing the observed biological responses.

As previously noted, 1,444 different comparisons between 38 bioindicators and 38 contaminants were assessed at α = 0.05 and thus about 72 results may be significant due to chance alone. Further study to determine whether the patterns observed between cellular parameters and contaminants are true relationships is warranted.

Conclusions

Food habits were noticeably different between ospreys nesting along the lower Duwamish River (LDR) and Willamette River (WR). LDR birds ate mostly hatchery-reared salmonids (captured in the LDR) during the pre-incubation period and soles (captured in the Puget Sound [PS]), peamouth (captured in Lake Washington [LW]), and salmonids (age 2–3+ year) (captured most often in the PS) during the nestling period while WR ospreys ate mostly

28

largescale suckers throughout the nesting period. Because LDR osprey food habits are largely comprised of hatchery-reared salmonids and other species captured outside of the Duwamish River, contaminants detected in osprey eggs do not accurately reflect current LDR contaminant burdens, and identifying the optimum avian species to monitor LDR contaminants that biomagnify up the food chain more effectively is problematic. Furthermore, contaminants detected in osprey nestling blood/plasma do not accurately reflect residues found in the LDR (nestlings also fed on fish captured outside the LDR) and are more reflective of the general central PS area and adjacent water body (LW). Although ospreys have been successfully used to monitor various rivers, estuaries and bays, this study demonstrates the difficulty in utilizing a top predator to monitor contaminants in a relatively small localized area (the LDR) within a larger estuarine system (PS) because of various alternative food resources and sites (ponds, lakes, hatchery released fish, etc.). Perhaps studies for monitoring contaminants using a translocated *in-situ* species (for example, Asian clam [*Corbicula fluminea*]) would better represent contaminant uptake and burdens in the LDR. The first record of osprey nesting along the LDR was from the early 1990s, following the 1983 initiation of a Washington Department Fish and Wildlife program to release yearling chinook salmon from the Icy Creek Hatchery (Rearing Ponds) on the Green-Duwamish River system to improve recreational fishing in the PS. The fact that these fish are (1) an ideal size (5–9 inches) for osprey capture and (2) are released during the same time frame that ospreys return from wintering areas to LDR nest sites (April–May) are likely important reasons that attracted ospreys to nest along the LDR.

The LDR and WR are influenced by different anthropogenic factors; the LDR is mostly industrial and the WR is primarily agricultural, inherently influencing the contaminant loads present in each system. Furthermore, the LDR has tidal influences and the WR river section where osprey nests were sampled does not. Osprey eggs from the LDR contained higher PCB residues as well as most other OCs, but lower PBDE residues than WR eggs; and in general, PCB residues as well as the majority of analyzed OCs in LDR osprey eggs have decreased significantly since 2003. Despite higher PCB concentrations in LDR osprey eggs than in WR eggs, residues in LDR eggs were less than known effect level concentrations to cause embryo mortality in eggs. The contaminants not analyzed in this study and/or the additive and synergistic effects of the various contaminants may have influenced the success of ospreys nesting on the LDR although further study is necessary to address the possible interactions, toxicities of mixtures, and effects (if any) on osprey behavior and reproductive potential.

Low globulin concentrations in LDR nestling blood plasma indicates that LDR nestlings may be immunologically compromised. Previous studies have reported that exposure to PCBs, even at low exposures, particularly relevant during the early stages of life, causes immunotoxicity, and that salmon from the Duwamish Waterway were immunosuppressed. Assessing the potential effects of contaminants on the health of osprey nestlings is complicated by the fact that baseline data for ospreys are not available and embryos that died prior to hatch and chicks that did not survive to sampling were not represented. If ospreys are immunosuppressed then contaminant concentrations lower than that known to cause effects would likely be of greater importance to the health and survival of ospreys. Furthermore, additive or synergistic relationships among contaminants would likely lower the concentration at which a contaminant(s) is toxic, which may be particularly relevant if an organism is immunologically compromised.

This was the first comprehensive study conducted with ospreys nesting along the LDR. Study results provide baseline contaminant data for LDR osprey eggs and nestling blood, osprey feeding habits, hematological and biochemical measurements in nestlings, and osprey and fish temporal and spatial contaminant patterns. Although study findings demonstrate the difficulty in using the osprey to monitor contaminants at a specific localized site in the PS (the LDR), results also identified significant differences in contaminant concentrations from osprey eggs collected at two distant PS locations (Snohomish River Estuary and the LDR in 2002–03) indicating that contaminant monitoring with osprey is useful for larger more general areas within the PS. Continued biomonitoring with ospreys in the PS will provide valuable information on general contaminant burdens and spatial and temporal patterns within the greater PS ecosystem as well as ecosystem function. To better understand the factors influencing the osprey population in the PS, subsequent studies should gather additional information on breeding adults (age, nutritional status, migratory patterns, reproductive potential), bald eagle disturbance, and residue data for other contaminants not analyzed in this study. Furthermore, future osprey studies should concentrate on identifying individuals (color banding) to provide specific biological information to better evaluate and assess the fitness of individuals, to evaluate and explore potential subtle changes in behavior (including reproductive behavior), and to determine long-term fate and return rates of individuals.

Acknowledgments

Partial funding was provided by the Elliott Bay Natural Resource Trustee Council (the National Oceanic and Atmospheric Administration, the Washington State Department of Fish and Wildlife, the Washington State Department of Ecology, the U.S. Fish and Wildlife Service, and the site's historic inhabitants, the Muckleshoot and Suquamish Indian Tribes) (2006–07) and the USGS Biomonitoring of Environmental Status and Trends (BEST) Program (2003–04). This study would not have been possible without assistance from several cooperators: Al Cummings (Port of Seattle), Mike Bates (Eagle Marine Services, Ltd.), Mike Bennett (Lehigh Northwest Cement Company), George Blomberg (Port of Seattle), Ela Esterberg (City of Seattle, Seattle City Light), Jim Gallis (David J. Joseph Co.), Kelly Garber (Eagle Marine Services, Ltd.), R. Kelly George (Nucor Steel Seattle, Inc.), Michael Grady (The Boeing Company), Larry Graham (Northland Services), Nick Halverson (King County Parks and Recreation Division), Bart Kale (Nucor Steel Seattle, Inc.), Michael Lueskow (Northland Services), Lee MacGregor (SSA Terminals), Richard Moralez (City of Seattle, Seattle City Light), and Eric Rangeloff (Seattle Transload, Inc.). Authors thank Jim Shannon (Senior Scientist, David Evans and Associates Inc., Bellevue, Washington) for assistance with fish identification, and Terence Lee and Susan Colbert (USFWS) for field assistance.

References Cited

Anchor Environmental L.L.C., 2005, Evaluation and assessment of hatchery and wild salmon interactions in WRIA 9: Seattle, Washington: Technical report prepared for WRIA 9 Steering Committee c/o King County, 87 p.

Arena, S.M., Halbrook, R.S., and Arena, C.A., 1999, Predicting starling chick carcass PCB concentrations from PCB concentrations in ingested animal matter: Archives of Environmental Contamination and Toxicology, v. 37, p. 548-553.

Arkoosh, M.R., Casillas, E., Clemons, E., McCain, B.B., and Varanasi, U., 1991, Suppression of immunological memory in juvenile Chinook salmon (*Oncorhynchus tshawytscha*) from an urban estuary: Fish and Shellfish Immunology, v. 1, p. 261-277.

Arkoosh, M.R., Casillas, E., Huffman, P., Clemons, E., Evered, J., Stein, J.E., and Varanasi, U., 1998, Increased susceptibility of juvenile Chinook salmon (*Oncorhynchus tshawytscha*) from a contaminated estuary to the pathogen Vibrio anguillarum: Transactions of the American Fisheries Society, v. 127, p. 360-374.

Balbontin, J., and Ferrer, M., 2002, Plasma chemistry reference values in free-living Bonelli's Eagle (*Hieraaetus Fasciatus*) nestlings: Journal of Raptor Research, v. 36, p. 231-235.

Barron, M.G., Galbraith, H., and Beltman, D., 1995, Comparative reproductive and developmental toxicity of PCBs in birds: Comparative Biochemistry and Physiology, v. 112C, p. 1-14.

Bierer, B.W., Thomas, J.B., Roebuck, D.E., Powell, H.S., and Eleazer, T.H., 1963, Hematocrit and sedimentation rate values as an aid in poultry disease diagnosis: Journal of the American Veterinary Medical Association, v. 143, p. 1096-1098.

Bird, D.M., Gautier, J., and Montpetit, V., 1984, Embryonic growth of American kestrels: The Auk, v. 101, p. 392-396.

Blom, S., and Förlin, L., 1997, Effects of PCB on xenobiotic biotransformation enzyme activities in the liver and 21-hydroxylation in the head kidney of juvenile rainbow trout: Aquatic Toxicology, v. 39, p. 215-230.

Blus, L.J, 1984, DDE in birds' eggs: Comparison of two methods for estimating critical levels: Wilson Bull, v. 96, p. 268-276.

Boal, C.W., Hudelson, K.S., Mannan, R.W., and Estabrook, T.S., 1998, Hematology and hematozoa of adult and nestling cooper's hawks in Arizona: Journal of Raptor Research, v. 32, p. 281-285.

Bosveld A.T.C., and Van den Berg, M., 1994, Effects of polychlorinated biphenyls, dibenzo-p-dioxins, and dibenzofurans on fish-eating birds: Environmental Reviews, v. 2, p. 147-166.

Bosveld, A.T.C., Gardner, J., Murk, A.J., Brouwer, A., Van Kampen, M., Evers, E.H.G., and Van den Berg, M., 1995, Effects of PCDDs, PCDFs, and PCBs in common tern (*Sterna hirundo*) breeding in estuarine and coastal colonies in the Netherlands and Belgium: Environmental Toxicology and Chemistry, v. 14, p. 99-115.

Bowerman, W.W., 1993, Regulation of bald eagle (*Haliaeetus leucocephalus*) productivity in the Great Lakes Basin: An ecological and toxicological approach: East Lansing, Michigan, Michigan State University, Ph.D. dissertation.

Bowerman, W.W., Giesy, J.P., Best, D.A., and Kramer, V.J., 1995, A review of factors affecting productivity of bald eagles in the Great Lakes region: Implications for recovery: Environmental Health Perspect, v. 103, p. 51-59.

Bowerman, W.W., Best, D.A., Grubb, T.G., Sikarskie, J.G., and Giesy, J.P., 2000a., Assessment of environmental endocrine disruptors in bald eagles of the Great Lakes: Chemosphere, v. 41, p. 1569-1574.

Bowerman, W.W., Stickle, J.E., Sikarskie, J.G., and Giesy, J.P., 2000b, Hematology and serum chemistries of nestling bald eagles (*Haliaeetus leucocephalus*) in the lower peninsula of MI, USA: Chemosphere, v. 41, p. 1575-1579.

Brouwer, A., Longnecker, M.P., Birnbaum, L.S., Cogliano, J., Kostyniak, P., Moore, J., Schantz, S., and Winneke, G., 1999, Characterization of potential endocrine-related health effects at low-dose levels of exposure to PCBs. Environ: Health Perspect, v. 107, p. 639-649.

Brunstorm, B., 1989, Toxicity of coplanar polychlorinated biphenyls in avian embryos: Chemosphere, v. 19, p. 765-768.

Brunstorm, B., and Reutergardh, L., 1986, Differences in sensitivity of some avian species to the embryotoxicity of a PCB, 3,3',4,4'-Tetrachlorobiphenyl, injected in to the eggs: Environmental Pollution, v. 42, p. 37-45.

Bush, B., Tumasonis, C.F., and Baker, F.D., 1974, Toxicity and persistence of PCB homologs and isomers in the avian system: Archives of Environmental Contamination and Toxicology, v. 2, p. 195-212.

Bustamante, J., and Travaini, A., 1994, Effects of keeping plasma frozen at -20°C on the concentrations of blood metabolites: Comparative Biochemistry and Physiology, v. 107(A), p. 661-664.

Campbell, T.W., 1995, Avian Hematology and Cytology: Ames, Iowa, Iowa State University Press, p. 20-34.

Campbell, T.W., and Dein, F.J., 1984, Avian Hematology: The Basics. Veterinary Clinics of North America: Small Animal Practice, v. 14, p. 223-248.

Casillas, E., McCain, B.B., Arkoosh, M.R., Stein, J.E., and Varanasi, U., 1997, Estuarine pollution and juvenile salmon health: Potential impact on survival, *in* Emmett, R.L., and Schiewe, M.H., eds., Estuarine and Ocean Survival of Northeastern Pacific Salmon: Proceedings of the workshop: Newport, Oregon, NOAA Technical Memorandum NMFS-NWFSC-29, p. 169-178.

Chaplin, S.B., Diesel, D.A., and Kasparie, J.A., 1984, Body temperature regulation in red-tailed hawks and great horned owls: responses to air temperature and food deprivation: Condor, v. 86, p. 175-181.

Chu, S., Henny, C.J., Kaiser, J.L., Drouillard, K.G., Haffner, G.D., and Letcher, R.J., 2007, Dacthal and chlorophenoxy herbicides and chlorothalonil fungicide in eggs of Osprey (*Pandion haliaetus*) from the Duwamish-Lake Washington-Puget Sound area of Washington state, USA: Environmental Pollution, v. 145, p. 374-381.

Clark, T.P., Norstrom, R.J., Fox, G.A., and Won, H.T., 1987, Dynamics of organochlorine compounds in herring gulls (*Larus argentatus*): II. A two-compartment model and data for ten compounds: Environmental Toxicology and Chemistry, v. 6, p. 547-559.

Cossu, C., Doyotte, A., Jacquin, M.C., Babut, M., Exinger, A., and Vasseur, P., 1997, Glutathione reductase, selenium-dependent glutathione peroxidase, glutathione levels, and lipid peroxidation in freshwater bivalves, *Unio tumidus*, as biomarkers of aquatic contamination in field studies: Ecotoxicology and Environmental Safety, v. 38, p. 122-131.

Custer, C.M., Custer, T.W., Dummer, P.M., and Munney, K.L., 2003, Exposure and effects of chemical contaminants on tree swallows nesting along the Housatonic River, Berkshire County, Massachusetts, USA, 1998-2000: Environmental Toxicology and Chemistry, v. 22, p. 1605-1621.

Dawson, R.D., and Bortolotti, G.R., 1997, Are avian hematocrits indicative of condition? American kestrels as a model: Journal of Wildlife Management, v. 61, p. 1297-1306.

de Solla, S.R., and Martin, P.A., 2009, PCB accumulation in osprey exposed to local sources in lake sediment: Environmental Pollution, v. 157, p. 347-355.

Donaldson, G.M., Shutt, J.L., and Hunter, P., 1999, Organochlorine contamination in bald eagle eggs and nestlings from the Canadian Great Lakes: Archives of Environmental Contamination and Toxicology, v. 36, p. 70-80.

Doyotte, A., Cossu, C., Jacquin, M.C., Babut, M., and Vasseur, P., 1997, Antioxidant enzymes, glutathione and lipid peroxidation of experimental or field exposure in the gills and the digestive gland of the freshwater bivalve *Unio tumidus*: Aquatic Toxicology, v. 39, p. 93-110.

Drent, R.H., and Daan, S., 1980, The prudent parent: energetic adjustments in avian breeding: Ardea, v. 68, p. 225-252.

Duncan, J.R., Prasse, K.W., and Mahaffey, E.A., 1994, Veterinary laboratory medicine: Clinical pathology: Ames, Iowa, Iowa State University Press, p. 20-151.

Environmental Coalition of South Seattle (ECOSS), 2008, Winter Newsletter, v. 4, n. 3. Available online: http://www.ecoss.org/business_overview.html. (Accessed December 10, 2008).

Eisler, R., 2000, Handbook of Chemical Risk Assessment, Health Hazards to Humans, Plants, and Animals, Volume 2 Organics: Boca Raton, Florida: CRC Press LLC Printing, p. 1-1500.

Eisler, R., and Belisle, A.A., 1996, Planer PCB Hazards to Fish, Wildlife, and Invertebrates: A Synoptic Review: *In* Contaminant Hazard Reviews Report (USA), no. 31, U.S. Department of Interior, National Biological Service, Washington, DC, USA p.1-62.

Elliott, J.E., Machmer, M.M., Henny, C.J., Wilson, L.K., and Norstrom, R.J, 1998, Contaminants in ospreys from the Pacific Northwest: I. Trends and patterns in polychlorinated dibenzo-p-dioxins and dibenzofurans in eggs and plasma: Archives of Environmental Contamination and Toxicology, v. 35, p. 620-631.

Elliott, J.E., Machmer, M.M., Wilson, L.K., and Henny, C.J., 2000, Contaminants in ospreys from the Pacific Northwest: II. Organochlorine pesticides, polychlorinated biphenyls, and mercury, 1991-1997: Archives of Environmental Contamination and Toxicology, v. 38, p. 93-106.

Elliott, J.E., Wilson, L.K., Henny, C.J., Trudeau, S.F., Leighton, F.A., Kennedy, S.W., and Cheng, K.M., 2001, Assessment of biological effects of chlorinated hydrocarbons in osprey chicks: Environmental Toxicology and Chemistry, v. 20, p. 866-879.

Elliott, J.E., Morrissey, C.A., Henny, C.J., Inzunza, E.R., and Shaw, P., 2007, Satellite telemetry and prey sampling reveal contaminant sources to Pacific Northwest ospreys: Ecological Applications., v. 17, p. 1223-1233.

Ewins, P.J., 1993, Pigeon Guillemot (*Cepphus columba*), The Birds of North America Online, Poole, A., ed., Ithaca, New York, Cornell Lab of Ornithology; Retrieved from the Birds of North America Online: http://bna.birds.cornell.edu/bna/species/049.

Fair, J., Whitaker, S., and Pearson, B., 2007, Sources of variation in haematocrit in birds: Ibis, v. 149, p. 535-552.

Fernie, K.J., Smits, J.E., Bortolotti, G.R., and Bird, D.M., 2001a, Reproduction success of American kestrels exposed to dietary polychlorinated biphenyls: Environmental Toxicology and Chemistry, v. 20, p. 776-781.

Fernie, K.J., Smith, J.E., Bortolotti, G.R., and Bird, D.M., 2001b, *In ovo* exposure to polychlorinated biphenyls: Reproductive effects on second-generation American kestrels: Archives of Environmental Contamination and Toxicology, v. 40, p. 544-550

Fernie, K., Bortolotti, G.R., and Smits, J., 2003, Reproductive abnormalities, teratogenicity, and developmental problems in American kestrels (*Falco sparverius*) exposed to polychlorinated biphenyls: Journal of Toxicology and Environmental Health: Part A, v. 66, p. 2089-2103.

Fernie, K.J., Mayne, G., Shutt, J.L., Pekarik, C., Grasman, K.A., Letcher, R.J., and Drouillard, K., 2005a, Evidence of immunomodulation in nestling American kestrels (*Falco sparverius*) exposed to environmentally relevant PBDEs: Environmental Pollution, v. 138, p. 485-493.

Fernie, K.J., Shutt, J.L., Mayne, G., Hoffman, D., Letcher, R.J., Drouillard, K.G., and Ritchie, I.J., 2005b, Exposure to Polybrominated Diphenyl Ethers (PBDEs): Changes in thyroid, vitamin a, glutathione homeostasis, and oxidative stress in American kestrels (*Falco sparverius*). Toxicological Science, v. 88, p. 375-383.

Ferrer, M., García-Rodríguez, T., Carrillo, J.C., and Castroviejo, J., 1987, Hematocrit and blood chemistry values in captive raptors: Comparative Biochemistry and Physiology, v. 87A, p. 1123-1127.

Friend, M., and Trainer, D.O., 1970, Polychlorinated biphenyl: Interaction with duck hepatitis virus: Science, v. 170, p. 1314-1316.

Fudge, A.M., 1997, Avian Clinical Pathology – Hematology and Chemistry, in Altman, R.B., Clubb, S.L., Dorrestein, G.M., and Quesenberry, K., eds., Avian Medicine and Surgery: Philadelphia, Pennsylvania, W.B. Saunders Company, p. 142-157.

García-Rodríguez, T., Ferrer, M., Carrillo, J.C., and Castroviejo, J., 1987a, Metabolic responses of Buteo buteo to long-term fasting and refeeding. Comparative Biochemistry and Physiology, v. 87A, p. 381-386.

García-Rodríguez, T., Ferrer, M., Recio, F., and Castroviejo, J., 1987b, Circadian rhythms of determined blood chemistry values in Buzzards and Eagle Owls: Comparative Biochemistry and Physiology, v. 88A, p. 663-669.

Gauthier, L.T., Hebert, C.E., Weseloh, D.V.C., and Letcher, R.J., 2008, Dramatic changes in the temporal trends of polybrominated diphenyl ethers (PBDEs) in herring gull eggs from the Laurentian Great Lakes: 1982-2006. Environmental Science and Technology, v. 42, p. 1524-1530.

Gee, G.F., Carpenter, J.W., and Heusler, G.L., 1981, Species differences in hematological values of captives cranes, raptors and quail: Journal of Wildlife Management, v. 45, p. 463-483.

Gilbertson, M., Kubiak, T.J., Ludwig, J.P., and Fox, G.A., 1991, Great Lakes embryo mortality, edema, and deformities syndrome (GLEMEDS) in colonial fish-eating birds: Similarity to chick-edema disease: Journal of Toxicology and Environmental Health, v. 33, p. 455-520.

Great Lakes Institute for Environmental Research (GLIER), 1995, Methods and procedures Quality Manual, 1st ed., O Revision: Ontario, Canada, University of Windsor.

Grasman, K.A., Fox, G.A., Scanlon, P.F., and Ludwig, J.P., 1996, Organochlorine-associated immunosuppression in prefledgling Caspian terns and herring gulls from the Great Lakes: An ecoepidemiological study: Environmental Health Perspectives, v. 104, p. 829-842.

Grasman, K.A., Armstrong, M., Hammersly, D.L., Scanlon, P.F., and Fox, G.A., 2000, Geographic variation in blood plasma protein concentrations in young herring gulls (*Larus argentatus*) and Caspian terns (*Sterna caspia*) from the Great Lakes and Winnipeg: Comparative Biochemistry and Physiology, v. 125C, p. 365-375.

Grasman, K.A., and Fox, G.A., 2001, Associations between altered immune function and organochlorine contamination in young Caspian terns (*Sterna caspia*) from Lake Huron, 1997-1999: Ecotoxicology, v. 10, p. 101-114.

Habig, W.H, Pabst, M.J., and Jacoby, W.B., 1974, Glutathione S-transferase: the first enzymatic step in mercapturic acid formation: The Journal of Biological Chemistry, v. 25, p. 7130-7139.

Halliwell, W.H., 1981, Serum chemistry profile in the health and disease of birds of prey: Proc of the International Symposium on Diseases of Birds of Prey: West Yorkshire, England: Chiron Publications, Ltd, p. 1-111.

Harr, K.E., 2002, Clinical chemistry of companion avian species: a review. Veterinary Clinical Pathology, v. 31, p. 140-151.

Haseltine, S.D., and Prouty, R.M., 1980, Aroclor 1242 and reproductive success of adult mallards (*Anas platyrhynchos*): Environmental Research, v. 23, p. 29-34.

Hebert, C.E, Norstrom, R.J., Simon, M., Braune, B.M., Weseloh, D.V., and McDonald, C.R., 1994, Temporal trends and sources of PCDDs and PCDFs in the Great Lakes: herring gull egg monitoring, 1981-1991: Environmental Science and Technology, v. 28, p. 1268-1277.

Henny, C.J., and Meeker, D.L., 1981, An evaluation of blood plasma for monitoring DDE in birds of prey: Environmental Pollution, v. 25A, p. 291-304.

Henny, C.J., Griffin, C.R., Stahlecker, D.W., Harmata, A.R., and Cromartie, E., 1981, Low DDT residues in plasma of bald eagles (*Haliaeetus leucocephalus*) wintering in Colorado and Missouri: Canadian Field-Naturalist, v. 95, p. 249-252.

Henny, C.J., Blus, L.J., and Stafford, C.J., 1983, Effects of heptachlor on American kestrels in the Columbia Basin, Oregon: Journal of Wildlife Management, v. 47, p. 1080-1087.

Henny, C.J., and Kaiser, J.L., 1996, Osprey population increase along the Willamette River, Oregon, and the role of utility structures, 1976-1993, *in* Bird, D.M., Varland, D.E., and Negro, J.J. (eds.), Raptors in Human Landscapes, London, Academic Press, Ltd., p. 97-108.

Henny, C.J., Kaiser, J.L. Grove, R.A. Bentley, V.R., and Elliott, J.E., 2003, Biomagnification factors (fish to osprey eggs from Willamette River, Oregon U.S.A.) for PCDDs, PCDFs, PCBs, and OC pesticides: Environmental Monitoring and Assessment, v. 84, p. 275-315.

Henny, C.J., Grove, R.A., Kaiser, J.L., and Bentley, V.R., 2004, An evaluation of osprey eggs to determine spatial residue patterns and effects of contaminants along the lower Columbia River, U.S.A.,. *in* Chancellor, R., and Meyburg, B. (eds.), Raptors Worldwide: Proceedings of the 6th World Conference on Birds of Prey and Owls, May 2003, Budapest, Hungary, WWGBP/MME, p. 369-388

Henny, C.J., Grove, R.A., and Kaiser, J.L., 2008, Osprey distribution, abundance, reproductive success and contaminant burdens along Lower Columbia River, 1997–1998 versus 2004: Archives of Environmental Contamination and Toxicology, v. 54, p. 525-534.

Henny, C.J., Kaiser, J.L., and Grove, R.A., 2009a, PCDDs, PCDFs, PCBs, OC pesticides and mercury in fish and osprey eggs from Willamette River, Oregon (1993, 2001, and 2006) with calculated biomagnifications factors: Ecotoxicology, v 18, p. 151-173.

Henny, C.J., Kaiser, J.L., Grove, R.A., Johnson, B.L., and Letcher, R.J., 2009b, Polybrominated diphenyl ether flame retardants in eggs may reduce reproductive success of ospreys in Oregon and Washington, USA: Ecotoxicology, available online: DOI 10.1007/s10646-009-0323-4.

Hill, E.F., Heath, R.G., Spann, J.W., and Williams, J.D., 1975, Lethal dietary toxicities of environmental pollutants to birds: U.S. Fish and Wildlife Service, Special Scientific Report – Wildlife No. 191.

Hochleithner, M., 1999, Biochemistries, *in* Ritchie, B.W., Harrison, G.J., and Harrison, L.R., eds., Avian Medicine: Principles and Application: Lake Worth, Florida, Wingers Publishing, p. 223-245.

Hoffman, D.J., Franson, J.C., Pattee, O.H., Bunck, C.M., and Murray, H.C., 1985, Biochemical and hematological effects of lead ingestion in nestling American kestrels: Comparative Biochemistry and Physiology, v. 80C, p. 431-439.

Hoffman, D.J., Rattner, B.A., Bunck, C.M., Krynitsky, A., Ohlendorf, H.M., and Lowe, R.W., 1986, Association between PCBs and lower embryonic weight in black-crowned night herons in San Francisco Bay: Journal of Toxicology and Environmental Health, v. 19, p. 383-391.

Hoffman, D.J., Franson, J.C., Pattee, O.H., Bunck, C.M., and Murray, H.C., 1987, Toxicity of paraquat in nestling birds: effects of plasma and tissue biochemistry in American kestrels: Archives of Environmental Contamination and Toxicology, v. 16, p. 177-183.

Hoffman, D.J., Melancon, M.J., Klein, P.N., Rice, C.P., Eisemann, J.D., Hines, R.K., Spann, J.W., and Pendleton, G.W., 1996a, Development toxicity of PCB 126 (3,3,4,4,5-pentachlorobuphenyl) in nestling American kestrels (*Falco sparverius*): Fundamental and Applied Toxicology, v. 34, p. 188-200.

Hoffman, D.J., Rice, C.P., and Kubiac, T.J., 1996b, PCBs and dioxins in birds, *in* Beyer, W.N., Heinz, G.H., and Redmon-Norwood, A.W., eds., Environmental Contaminants in Wildlife: Interpreting Tissue Concentrations: Boca Raton, Florida, CRC/Lewis Publishers, p. 165-207.

Hoffman, D.J., and Heinz, G.H., 1998a, Effects of mercury (Hg) and selenium (Se) on glutathione metabolism and oxidative stress in mallard ducks: Environmental Toxicology and Chemistry, v. 17, p. 161-166.

Hoffman, D.J., Melancon, M.J., Klein, P.N., Eisemann, J.D., and Spann, J.W., 1998b, Comparative developmental toxicity of planar polychlorinated biphenyl congeners in chickens, American kestrels, and common terns: Environmental Toxicology and Chemistry, v. 17, p. 747-757.

Hudson River Natural Resource Trustees, 2004, Hudson River Natural Resource Damage Assessment – Data report for the collection of eggs from Spotted Sandpipers, American Woodcock, Belted Kingfisher, American Robin, Red-Winged Blackbird and Eastern Phoebe associated with the Hudson River from Hudson Falls to Schodack Island, New York Revised June 2005: Silver Spring, Maryland, Appendix A. U.S. Department of Commerce.

International Species Information System, 1983 *Haliaeetus Leucocephalus* (Bald eagle). Available online: www.isis.org/CMSHOME/. (Accessed March 2002).

Jain, N.C., 1993, Essentials of veterinary hematology, Mundorff, G.H. ed.: Philadelphia, Pennsylvania, Lea and Febiger, p. 159-257.

Johnson, A., Seiders, K., Deligeannis, C., Kinney, K., Sandvik, P., Era-Miller, B., and Alkire, D., 2006, PBDE flame retardants in Washington Rivers and Lakes: Concentrations in fish and water, 2005-06: Olympia, Washington, Washington State Department of Ecology, Watershed Ecology Section Environmental Assessment Program, 98504-7710.

Johnson, B.L., Kaiser, J.L., Henny, C.J., and Grove, R.A., 2008, Prey of nesting ospreys on the Willamette and Columbia Rivers, Oregon and Washington: Northwest Science, v. 82, p. 229-236.

Johnson, L.L., Landahl, J.T., Kubin, L.A., Horness, B.H., Myers, M.S., Collier, T.K., and Stein, J.E., 1998, Assessing the effects of anthropogenic stressors on Puget Sound flatfish populations: Journal of Sea Research, v. 39, p. 125-137.

Johnson, L.L., Collier, T.K., and Stein, J.E., 2002, An analysis in support of sediment quality thresholds for polycyclic aromatic hydrocarbons (PAHs) to protect estuarine fish. Aquatic Conserv.: Mar. Freshw. Ecosyst., v. 12, p. 517-538.

Johnson, L.L., Ylitalo, G.M., Arkoosh, M.R., Kagley, A.N., Stafford, C., Bolton, J.L., Buzitis, J., Anulacion, B.F., and Collier, T.K., 2007, Contaminant exposure in outmigrant juvenile salmon from Pacific Northwest estuaries of the United States: Environmental Monitoring and Assessment, v. 124, p. 167-194.

Jones, M.P., 1999, Avian Clinical Pathology: Veterinary Clinics of North America, Exotic Animal Practice, v. 2, n. 3, p. 663-687.

Joseph, V., 1999, Raptor hematology and chemistry evaluation: Veterinary Clinics of North America, Exotic Animal Practice, v. 2, n. 3, p. 689-699.

Kannan, N., Reusch, T.B.H., Schulz-Bull, D.E., Petrick, G., and Duinker, J.C., 1995, Chlorobiphenyls: Model compounds for metabolism in food chain organisms and their potential use as ecotoxicological stress indicators by application in the metabolic slope concept: Environmental Science and Technology, v. 29, p. 1851-1859.

Krausmann, J.D., 2002, Preliminary exposure assessment of dioxin-like chlorobiphenyls in great blue herons of the lower Duwamish River in Seattle, Washington: Lacey, Washington, U.S. Fish and Wildlife Service, 19 p.

Kuiken, T., Fox, G.A., and Danesik, K.L., 1999, Bill malformations in double-crested cormorants with low exposure to organochlorines: Environmental Toxicology and Chemistry, v. 18, p. 2908-2913.

Laetz, C.A., Baldwin, D.H., Collier, T.K., Hebert, V., Stark, J.D., and Scholz, N.L., 2009, The synergistic toxicity of pesticide mixtures: implications for risk assessment and the conservation of the endangered Pacific salmon: Environmental Health Perspectives, v. 117, p. 348-353.

Larson, J.M., Karasov, W.H., Sileo, L., Stromborg, K.L., Hanbidge, B.A., Geisy, J.P., Jones, P.D., Tillitt, D.E., and Verbrugge, D.A., 1996, Reproductive success, developmental abnormalities, and environmental contaminants in Double-crested Cormorants (*Phalacrocorax auritus*): Environmental Toxicology and Chemistry, v. 15, p. 553-559.

Larzar, R., Edwards, R.C., Metcalfe, C.D., Metcalfe, T., Gobas, F.A., and Haffner, G.D., 1992, A simple, novel method for the quantitative analysis of coplanar (non-ortho substituted) polychlorinated biphenyls in environmental samples: Chemosphere, v. 25, p. 493-504.

Lanzarot, M.P., Montesinos, A., San Andrés, M.I., Rodríguez, C., and Barahona, M.V., 2001, Hematological, protein electrophoresis and cholinesterase values of free-living nestling peregrine falcons in Spain: Journal of Wildlife Diseases, v. 37, p. 172-177.

Leveille, G.A., and Sauberlich, H.E., 1961, Influence of dietary protein level on serum protein components and cholesterol in the growing chick: Journal of Nutrition, v. 74, p. 500-504.

Lounsbury-Billie, M.J., Rand, G.M., Cai, Y., and Bass, O.L., Jr., 2008, Metal concentrations in osprey (*Pandion haliaetus*) populations in the Florida Bay estuary: Ecotoxicology, v. 17, p. 616-622.

Ludwig, J.P., Auman, H.J., Kurita, H., Ludwig, M.E., Campbell, L.M., Giesy, J.P., Tillitt, D.E., Jones, P., and Yamashita, N., 1993, Caspian tern reproduction in the Saginaw Bay ecosystem following a 100-year flood event: Journal of Great Lakes Research, v. 19, p. 96-108.

Lumeij, J.T., 1994, Hepatology, *in* Ritchie, B.W., Harrison, G.J., Harrison, L.R., eds., Avian Medicine: Principles and Application: Lake Worth, Florida, Wingers Publishing, p. 522-537.

Macnamara, M., 1972, Sexing the American Osprey using secondary sexual characteristics, *in* Ogden, J.C., ed., North American Osprey Research Conference: Transactions of the North American Osprey Research Conference, February 1972, College of William and Mary, Williamsburg, Virginia, p. 43-45.

Malins, D.C., McCain, B.B., Brown, D.W., Chan, S.L., Myers, M.S., Landahl, J.T., Prohaska, P.G., Friedman, A.J., Rhodes, L.D., Burrows, D.G., Gronlund, W.D., and Hodgins, H.O., 1984, Chemical pollutants in sediments and diseases of bottom-dwelling fish in Puget Sound, Washington: Environmental Science and Technology, v. 18, p. 705-713.

Malins, D.C., McCain, B.B., Myers, M.S., Brown, M.S., Krahn, M.M., Roubal, W.T., Schiewe, M.H., Landahl, J.T., and Chan, S.L., 1987, Field and laboratory studies of the etiology of liver neoplasms in marine fish from Puget Sound: Environmental Health Perspectives, v. 71, p. 5-16.

Mallory, M., and Metz, K., 1999, Common Merganser (*Mergus merganser*), The Birds of North America Online (A. Poole, ed.), Ithaca: Cornell Lab of Ornithology; Retrieved from the Birds of North America Online: http://bna.birds.cornell.edu/bna/species/442

Martin, P.A., de Solla, S.R., and Ewins, P., 2003, Chlorinated hydrocarbon contamination in osprey eggs and nestlings from the Canadian Great Lakes Basin, 1991-1995: Ecotoxicology, v. 12, p. 209-224.

Mauro, L., 1987, Hematology and blood chemistry, *in* Giron, B.A., Pedleton, B.A., Millsap, Cline, K.W., and Bird, D.M., eds., Raptor Management Techniques Manual, National Wildlife Federation, Washington, D.C., p. 269-276.

McCain, B.B., Malins, D.C., Krahn, M.M., Brown, D.W., Gronlund, W.D., Moore, L.K., and Chan, SL., 1990, Uptake of aromatic and chlorinated hydrocarbons by juvenile chinook salmon (*Oncorhynchus tshawytscha*) in an urban estuary: Archives of Environmental Contamination and Toxicology, v. 19, p. 10-16.

McCarty, J.P., and Secord, A.L., 1999a, Reproductive ecology of Tree Swallows (*Tachycineta bicolor*) with high levels of polychlorinated biphenyl contamination: Environmental Toxicology and Chemistry, v. 18, p. 1433-1439.

McCarty, J.P., and Secord, A.L., 1999b, Nest-building behavior in PCB-contaminated Tree Swallows: Auk, v. 116, p. 55-63.

Meador, J.P., Collier, T.K., and Stein, J.E., 2002, Use of tissue and sediment-based threshold concentrations of polychlorinated biphenyls (PCBs) to protect juvenile salmonids listed under the Endangered Species Act: Aquatic Conservation: Marine and Freshwater Ecosystems, v. 12, p. 493-516.

Mealey, B., Parks, G.M., Pages, C.M., Millsap, B.A., Bass, O.L., and Bossart, G.D., 2004, Serum chemistry values for nestling bald eagles (*Haliaeetus Leucocephalus*) in Florida Bay, Everglades National Park: Journal of Raptor Research, v. 38, p. 96-100.

Meister, A., 1988, Glutathione metabolism and its selective modification: Journal of Biological Chemistry, v. 263, p. 17205-17208.

McKinney, M.A., Cesh, L.S., Elliott, J.E., Williams, T.D., Garcelon, D.K., and Letcher, R.J., 2006, Brominated flame retardants and halogenated phenolic compounds in North American west coast bald eaglet (*Haliaeetus leucocephalus*) plasma: Environmental Science and Technology, v. 40, p. 6275-6281.

Myers, M.S., Landahl, J.T., Krahn, M.M., and McCain, B.B., 1991, Relationships between hepatic neoplasms and related lesions and exposure to toxic chemicals in marine fish from the U.S. West Coast: Environmental Health Perspectives, v. 90, p. 7-15.

Myers, M.S., Johnson, L.L., and Collier, T.K., 2003, Establishing the causal relationship between polycyclic aromatic hydrocarbons (PAH) exposure and hepatic neoplasms and neoplasia-related liver lesions in English sole (*Pleuronectes vetulus*): Human and Ecological Risk Assessment, v. 9, p. 67-94.

Newman, S.H., Piatt, J.F., and White, J., 1997, Hematological and plasma biochemical reference ranges of Alaskan seabirds: Their ecological significance and clinical importance: Colonial Waterbirds, v. 20, p. 492-504.

Newton, I., 1979, Population Ecology of Raptors: Vermilion South Dakota, Buteo Books, 399 p.

National Marine Fisheries Service, 2002, Washington Department of Fish and Wildlife Hatchery and Genetic Management Plan, Soos Creek / Icy Creek Fall Chinook Yearling Program, 33 p.

Norstrom, R.J., Clark, T.P., Jeffrey, D.A., Won, H.T., and Gilman, A.P., 1986, Dynamics of organochlorine compounds in herring gulls (*Larus argentatus*): Distribution and clearance of [14C]DDE in free-living herring gulls: Environmental Toxicology and Chemistry, v. 5, p. 41-48.

Norstrom, R.J., Simon, M., Moisey, J., Wakeford, B., and Weseloh, D.V.C., 2002, Geographical distribution (2000) and temporal trends (1981-2000) of brominated diphenyl ethers in Great Lakes herring gull eggs: Environmental Science and Technology, v. 36, p. 4783-4789.

Okumura, J., and Tasaki, I., 1969, Effect of fasting, refeeding and dietary protein levels on uric acid and ammonia content of blood, liver and kidney in chickens: Journal of Nutrition, v. 97, p. 316-320.

O'Neill, S.M., West, J.E., and Hoeman, J.C., 1998, Spatial trends in the concentration of polychlorinated biphenyls (PCBs) in Chinook (*Oncorhynchus tshawytscha*) and Coho salmon (*O. kisutch*) in Puget Sound and factors affecting PCB accumulations: Results from the Puget Sound Ambient Monitoring Program, *in* Strickland, E.R., ed., Puget Sound Research '98 Proceedings: Seattle, Washington, Puget Sound Water Quality Action Team, p. 312-328.

Peakall, D.B., and Peakall, M.L., 1973, Effects of polychlorinated biphenyl on the reproduction of artificially and naturally incubated dove eggs: Journal of Applied Ecology, v. 10, p. 863-868.

Perry, W.B., 2008, Everglades restoration and water quality challenges in south Florida: Ecotoxicology, v. 17, p. 569-578.

Polo, F.J., Celdrán, J.F., Peinado, V.I., Viscor, G., and Palomeque, J., 1992, Hematological values for four species of birds of prey: Condor, v. 94, p. 1007-1013.

Poole, A.F., 1989, Ospreys – A natural and unnatural history: Cambridge, New York: Cambridge University Press, p. 1-246.

Poole, A.F., Bierregaard, R.O., and Martell, M.S., 2002, Osprey (*Pandion haliaetus*), The Birds of North America Online: Ithaca, New York, Cornell Lab of Ornithology; Retrieved from the Birds of North America Online: http://bna.birds.cornell.edu/bna/species/683.

Postupalsky, S., 1974, Raptor reproductive success: some problems with methods, criteria, and terminology, *in* Hamerstrom, F.N., Jr., Harrell, B.E., and Ohlendorff, R.R., eds., Management of Raptors, Proceedings of Conference on Raptor Conservation Techniques, Raptor Research Report No. 2, p. 21-31.

Postupalsky, S., 1977, A critical review of problems in calculating osprey reproductive success, *in* Ogden, J.C., ed.: Washington, D.C., Transactions No. American Osprey Research Conference., Transations and Proceedings. Series, No. 2, Natl. Park Serv., p. 1-11.

Powell, D.C., Aulerich, R.J., Meadows, J.C., Tillitt, D.E., Giesy, J.P., Stromborg, K.L., and Bursian, S.J., 1996, Effects of 3,3',4,4',5-pentachlorobiphenyl (PCB 126) and 2,3,7,8-tetrachlorodibenzo-p-dioxin (TCDD) injected into the yolks of chicken (*Gallus domesticus*) eggs prior to incubation: Archives of Environmental Contamination and Toxicology, v. 31, p. 404-409.

Powell, D.C, Aulerich, R.J., Meadows, J.C., Tillitt, D.E., Kelly, M.E., Stromborg, K.L., Melancon, M.J., Fitzgerald, S.D., and Bursian, S.J., 1998, Effects of 3,3',4,4',5-pentachlorobiphenyl and 2,3,7,8-tetrachlorodibenzo-p-dioxin injected into the yolks of double-crested cormorant (*Phalacrocorax auritus*) eggs prior to incubation: Environmental Toxicology and Chemistry, v. 17, p. 2035-2040.

Raldúa, D., Padrós, F., Solé, M., Eljarrat, E., Barceló, D., Riva, M.C., and Barata, C., 2008, First evidence of polybrominated diphenyl ether (flame retardants) effects in feral barbel from the Ebro River basin (NE, Spain): Chemosphere, v. 73, p. 56-64.

Rattner, B.A., McGowan, P.C., Golden, N.H., Hatfield, J.S., Toschik, P.C., Lukei, R.F., Jr., Hale, R.C., Schmitz-Alfonso, I., and Rice, C.P., 2004, Contaminant exposure and reproductive success of osprey (*Pandion haliaetus*) nesting in Chesapeake Bay regions of concern. Archives of Environmental Contamination and Toxicology, v. 47, p. 126-140.

Rattner, B., Golden, N., Toschik, P., McGowan, P., and Custer, T., 2008, Concentrations of metals in blood and feathers of nestling osprey (*Pandion haliaetus*) in Chesapeake and Delaware Bays: Archives of Environmental Contamination and Toxicology, v. 54, p. 114-122.

Rayne, S., Ikonomou, M.G., and Antcliffe, B., 2003, Rapidly increasing polybrominated diphenyl ether concentrations in the Columbia River system from 1992 to 2000: Environmental Science and Technology, v. 37, p. 2847-2854.

Redig, P.T., Mauro, L., Duke, G.E., and Frenzel, L.D., 1983, Towards better methods in assessing clinical problems of bald eagles: II. Serum chemistry, *in* Bird, D.M., ed., Biology and Management of Bald Eagles and Ospreys: Anne de Bellevue, Quebec, Harpell Press, Ste.

Rehder, N.B., Bird, D.M., Lague, P.C., and Mackay, C., 1982, Variation in selected hematological parameters of captive red-tailed hawks: Journal of Wildlife Distribution, v. 18, p. 105-109.

Sagerup, K., Henriksen, E.O., Skorping, A., Skaares, J.U., and Gabrielsen, G.W., 2000, Intensity of parasitic nematodes increases with organochlorine levels in the glaucous gull: Journal of Applied Ecology, v. 37, p. 532-539.

SAS Institute, 2003, SAS User's Guide: Statistics, Version 9.1 Edition, SAS Inst., Inc., Cary, NC.

Schaadt, C.P., and Bird, D.M., 1993, Sex-specific growth in ospreys: the role of sexual size dimorphism: Auk, v. 110, p. 900-910.

Smith, E.E., and Bush, M., 1978, Haematologic parameters on various species of strigiformes and falconiformes: Journal of Wildlife Distribution, v. 14, p. 447-450.

Spitzer, P.R., 1980, Dynamics of a discrete coastal breeding population of Ospreys in the northeastern United States during the period of decline and recovery, 1969-1978: Ithaca, New York, Cornell University, Ph.D. Thesis.

Spitzer, P.R., Pool, A.F., and Schebel, M., 1983, Initial recovery of breeding Ospreys in the region between New York City and Boston, *in* Bird, D.M., ed., Biology and Management of Bald Eagles and Ospreys: Anne de Bellevue, Quebec: Harpell Press, Ste., p. 231-241.

Stickel, L.F., Wiemeyer, S.N. and Blus, L.J., 1973, Pesticide residues in eggs of wild birds: Adjustment for loss of moisture and lipid. Bulletin of Environmental Contamination and Toxicology, v. 9, p. 193-196.

Stotts, V.D., and Henny, C.J., 1975, The age at first flight of young American Ospreys: Wilson Bulletin, v. 87, p. 277-278.

Stow, C.A., 1995, Great Lakes herring gull egg PCB concentrations indicate approximate steady-state conditions: Environmental Science and Technology, v. 29, p. 2893-2897.

Stein, J.E., Hom, T., Collier, T.K., Brown, D.W., and Varanasi, W., 1995, Contaminate exposure and biochemical effects in outmigrant juvenile Chinook salmon from urban and nonurban estuaries of Puget Sound, Washington: Environmental Toxicology and Chemistry, v. 14, p. 1019-1029.

Sturkie, P.D., 2000, Avian Physiology (5th ed.), Whittow, G.C., ed.: San Diego, California, Academic Press.

Summer, C.L., Giesy, J.P., Bursian, S.J., Render, J.A., Kubiak, T.J., Jones, P.D., Verbrugge, D.A., and Aulerich, R.J., 1996, Effects induced by feeding organochlorine-contaminated carp from Saginaw Bay, Lake Huron, to laying White Leghorn hens. II. Embryotoxic and teratogenic effects: Journal of Toxicology and Environmental Health, v. 49, p. 409:438.

Tatum, L.M., Zaias, A., Mealey, B.K., Cray, C., and Bossart, G.D., 2000, Protein electrophoresis as a diagnostic and prognostic tool in raptor medicine: Journal of Zoo Wildlife Medicine, v. 31, p. 497-502.

Thomas, J.S., 2000, Overview of plasma proteins, in Schalm's Veterinary Hematology (5th ed.), Feldman, B.F., Zinkl, J.G., and Jain, N.C., eds.: Baltimore, Maryland, Lippincott Williams and Wilkins.

Tori, G.M., and Peterle, T.J., 1983, Effects of PCBs on mourning dove courtship behavior. Bulletin of environmental contamination and toxicology, v. 30, p. 44-49.

Toschik, P.C., Rattner, B.A., McGowan, P.C., Christman, M.C., Carter, D.B, Hale, R.C., Matson, C.W., and Ottinger, M.A., 2005, Effects of contaminant exposure on reproductive success of osprey (*Pandion haliaetus*) nesting in Delaware River and Bay, USA: Environmental Toxicology and Chemistry, v. 24, p. 617-628.

Totzke, U., Fenske, M., Hüppop, O., Raabe, H., and Schach, N., 1999, The influence of fasting on blood and plasma composition of herring gulls (*Larus argentatus*): Physiological and Biochemical Zoology, v. 72, p. 426-437.

Twiest, G., and Smith, C.J., 1970, Circadian rhythms in blood glucose level of chickens: Comparative Biochemistry and Physiology, v. 32, p. 371-375.

U.S. Environmental Protection Agency, 2001, NPL Site Narrative for Lower Duwamish Waterway: Seattle, Washington, Federal Register Notice September 13, 2001, Available online: http://www.epa.gov/superfund/sites/npl/nar1622.htm (accessed 9 January 2008).

U.S. Geological Survey, National Water Information System: Web Interface. USGS 12113350 Green River at Tukwila, WA. Available online: http://waterdata.usgs.gov/usa/nwis (Accessed December 4, 2008).

Van den Berg, M., Birnbaum, L., Bosveld, A.T.C., Brunström, B., Cook, P., Feeley, M., Giesy, J.P., Hanberg, A., Hasegawa, R., Kennedy, S.W., Kubiak, T., Larsen, J.C., Leeuwen, F.X., Liem, A.K., Nolt, C., Peterson, P.E., Poellinger, L., Safe, S., Schrenk, D., Tillitt, D., Tysklind, M., Younes, M., Waern, F., and Zacharewski, T., 1998, Toxic equivalency factors (TEFs) for PCBs, PCDDs, PCDFs for humans and wildlife: Environmental Health Perspectives, v. 160, p. 775-792.

Varanasi, U., Casillas, E., Arkoosh, M.R., Hom, T., Misitano, D., Brown, D.W., Chan, S., Collier, T.K., McCain, B.B., and Stein, J.E., 1993, Contaminant exposure and associated biological effects in juvenile Chinook salmon (*Oncorhynchus tshawytscha*) from urban and nonurban estuaries of Puget Sound, Washington, U.S. Dept. of Commerce, NOAA Tech. Memo., NMFS-NWFSC-8, 112 p.

Werner, L.L., and Reavill, D.R., 1999, The Diagnostic utility of serum protein electrophoresis. Veterinary Clinics of North America: Exotic Animal Practice, v. 2, n. 3, p. 651-662.

Wiemeyer, S.N., Bunck, C.M., and Krynitsky, A.J., 1988, Organochlorine pesticides, polychlorinated biphenyls and mercury in osprey eggs – 1970-1979 – and their relationships to shell thinning and productivity: Archives of Environmental Contamination and Toxicology, v. 17, p.767-787.

Windward, 2003, Lower Duwamish Waterway remedial investigation, Phase 1 remedial investigation report, Prepared for Lower Duwamish Waterway Group: Seattle, Washington, Windward Environmental LLC.

Windward, 2004, Lower Duwamish Waterway remedial investigation, Juvenile Chinook salmon data report final, May 21, 2004, Prepared for Lower Duwamish Waterway Group: Seattle, Washington, Windward Environmental LLC.

Windward, 2005a, Lower Duwamish Waterway remedial investigation, Fish and Crab Tissue Collection and Chemical Analyses, Final, July 27, 2005, Prepared for Lower Duwamish Waterway Group: Seattle, Washington, Windward Environmental LLC.

Windward, 2005b, Lower Duwamish Waterway remedial investigation, Fish and Crab Data Report Addendum: PCB congener data, MS/MSD analyses, and DDT confirmation Final, October 24, 2005, Prepared for Lower Duwamish Waterway Group: Seattle, Washington, Windward Environmental LLC.

Windward, 2006, Lower Duwamish Waterway remedial investigation, Data report: fish and crab tissue samples collected in 2005. Prepared for Lower Duwamish Waterway Group: Seattle, Washington, Windward Environmental LLC.

Windward, 2007a, Lower Duwamish Waterway remedial investigation, Phase 2 Remedial Investigation Report, Appendix A: Baseline Ecological Risk Assessment, Final Report, July 31, 2007, Prepared for Lower Duwamish Waterway Group: Seattle, Washington, Windward Environmental LLC.

Windward, 2007b, Lower Duwamish Waterway remedial investigation, Remedial Investigation Report, Draft, November 5, 2007, Prepared for Lower Duwamish Waterway Group: Seattle, Washington, Windward Environmental LLC.

Yamashita, N., Shimada, T., Ludwig, J.P., Kurita, H., Ludwig, M.E., and Tatsukawa, R., 1993, Embryonic abnormalities and organochlorine contamination in double-crested cormorants (*Phalacrocorax auritus*) and Caspian terns (*Hydroprogne caspia*) from the upper Great Lakes in 1988: Environmental Pollution, v. 79, p. 163-173.

Zar, J.H., 1999, Biostatistical Analysis: Upper Saddle River, New Jersey, Prentice Hall.

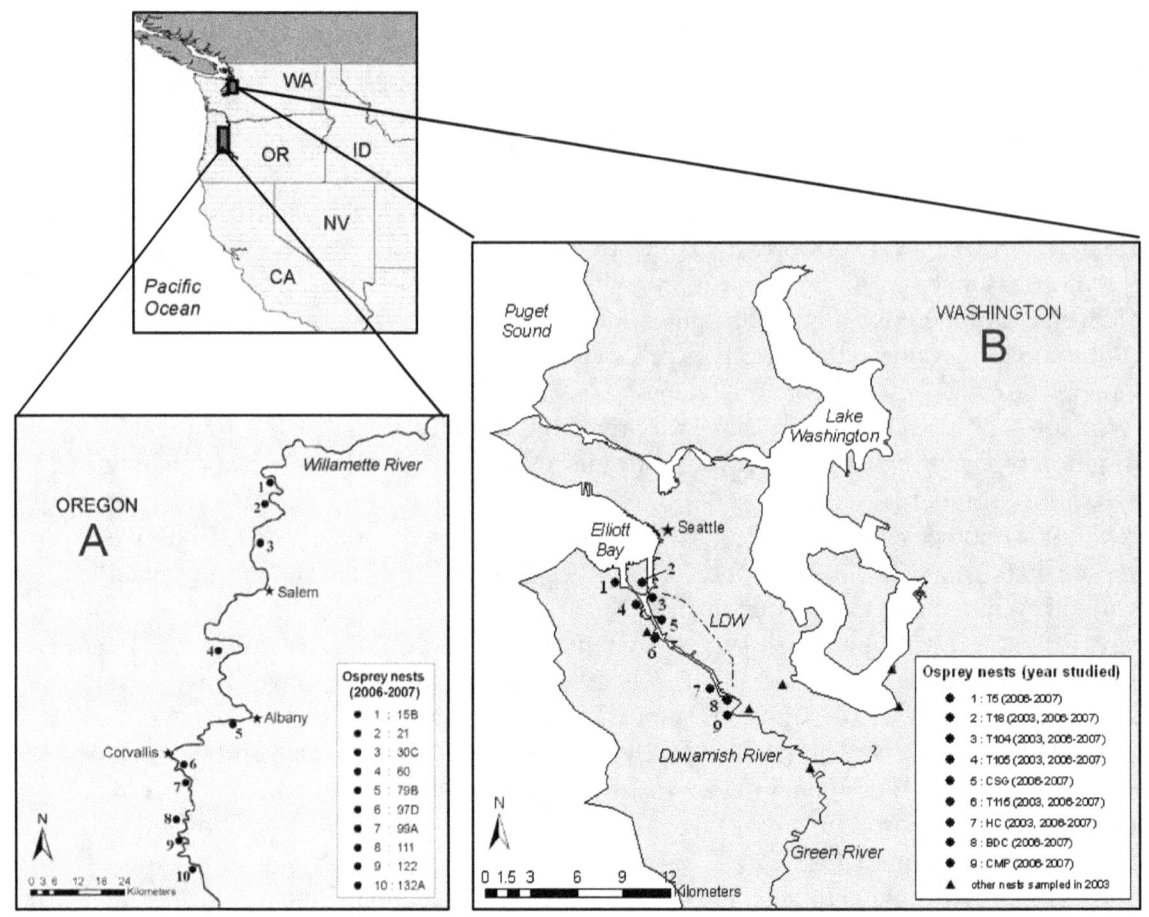

Map ID	Nest ID	River Kilometer (River Mile)	Egg Collected			Plasma Collected		# of Young Produced		
			2003	2006	2007	2006	2007	2003	2006	2007
A-1	15B	98.5 (61.2)		x		x			2	3
A-2	21	106.5 (66.2)		x		x			1	2
A-3	30C	121.0 (75.2)		x		x			1	3
A-4	60	168.2 (104.5)		x					1	2
A-5	79B	192.8 (119.8)		x		x			2	3
A-6	97D	217.7 (135.3)		x					2	2
A-7	99A	221.9 (137.9)		x					3	2
A-8	111	234.8 (145.9)		x		x			2	2
A-9	122	244.1 (151.7)		x		x			1	1
A-10	132A	253.1 (157.3)		x					0	2
B-1	T5	0.0							0	0
B-2	T18	0.0	x	x	x		x	2	0	2
B-3	T104	0.2 (0.1)		x	x		x	0	0	2
B-4	T105	0.6 (0.4)	x		x			2	0	0
B-5	CSG	1.6 (1.0)		x		x			2	2
B-6	T115	2.4 (1.5)	x	x		x		2	2	3
B-7	HC	7.1 (4.4)	x	x		x		2	2	2
B-8	BDC	7.9 (4.9)		x		x			2	2
B-9	CMP	9.2 (5.7)		x	x		x		2	2

Figure 1. Osprey nest sites studied and monitored; A = reference site Willamette River (WR), Oregon and B = lower Duwamish River (LDR), Washington. Map does not include nests in the Snohomish River Estuary (SRE) (farther north) sampled in 2002–03. Additional nests monitored along the LDR in 2003 only are not included in associated table.

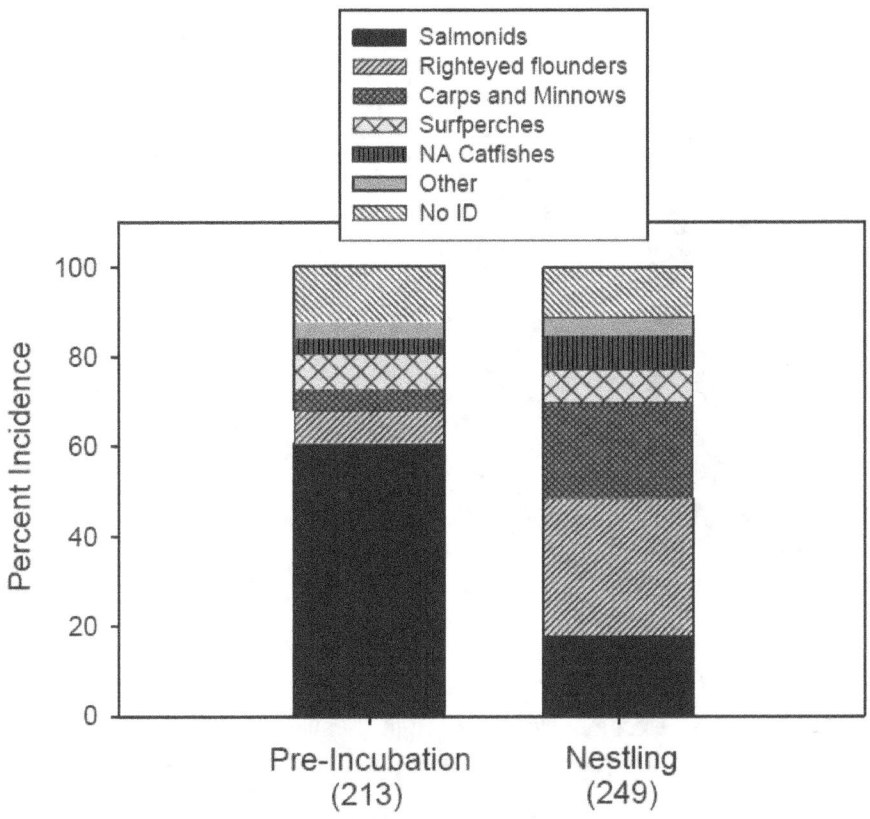

Figure 2. Percent incidence of fish families captured by ospreys nesting along the lower Duwamish River during selected nesting periods in 2006–07. Sample size shown in parentheses. Other category includes herrings (N =1), sculpins (N = 9), smelts (N = 5), perches (N = 2), suckers (N =1), and ratfishes (N = 1).

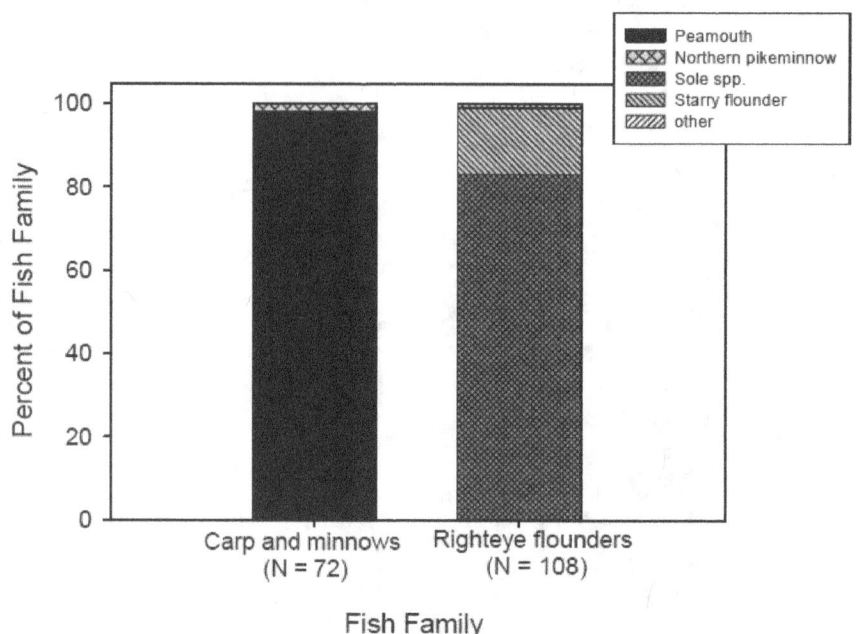

Figure 3. Frequency of species comprising selected fish families captured by ospreys nesting along the lower Duwamish River during the entire nesting period, 2006–07.

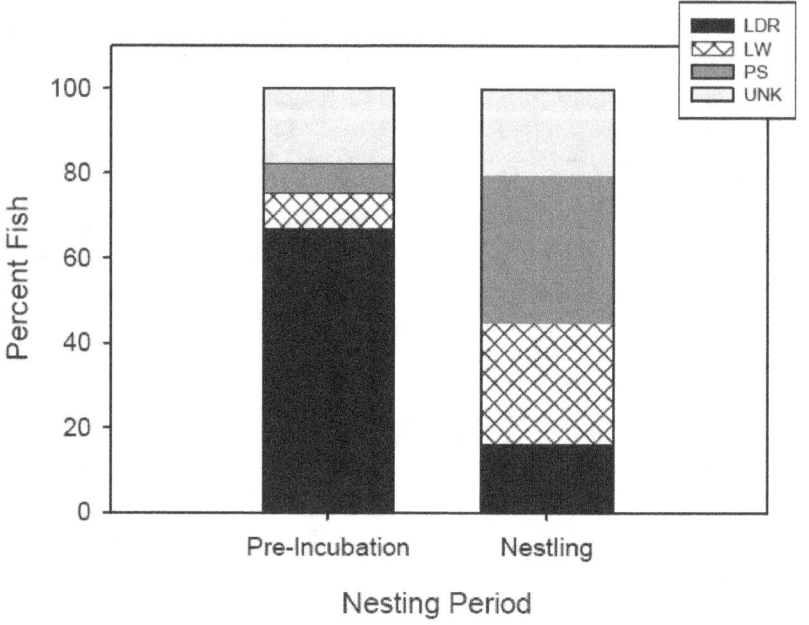

Figure 4. Percent fish captured in the lower Duwamish River (LDR), Lake Washington (LW), Puget Sound (PS) including Elliott Bay, and unknown (UNK) location by osprey nesting along the lower Duwamish River (2006–07) during selected nesting periods.

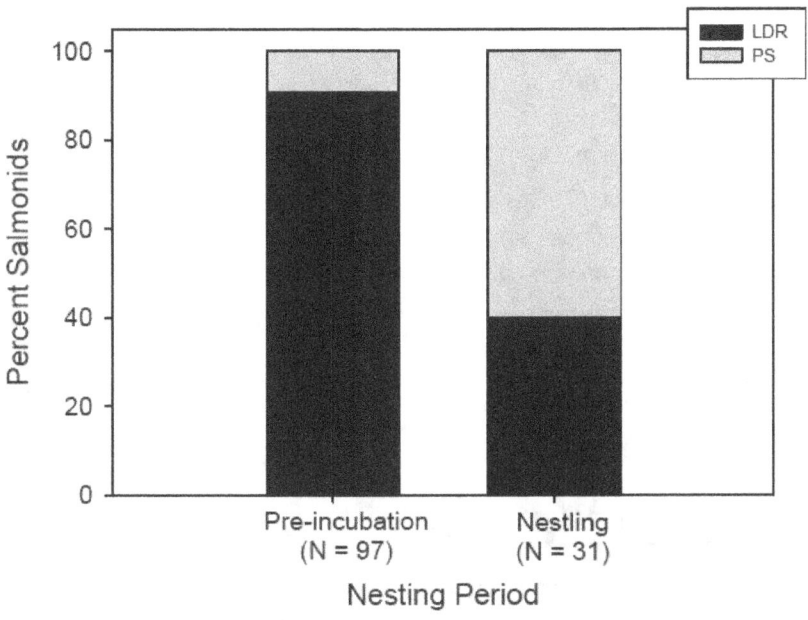

Figure 5. Frequency of salmonids captured in the lower Duwamish River (LDR) and Puget Sound (PS), Washington by ospreys nesting along the LDR during selected nesting periods, 2006–07.

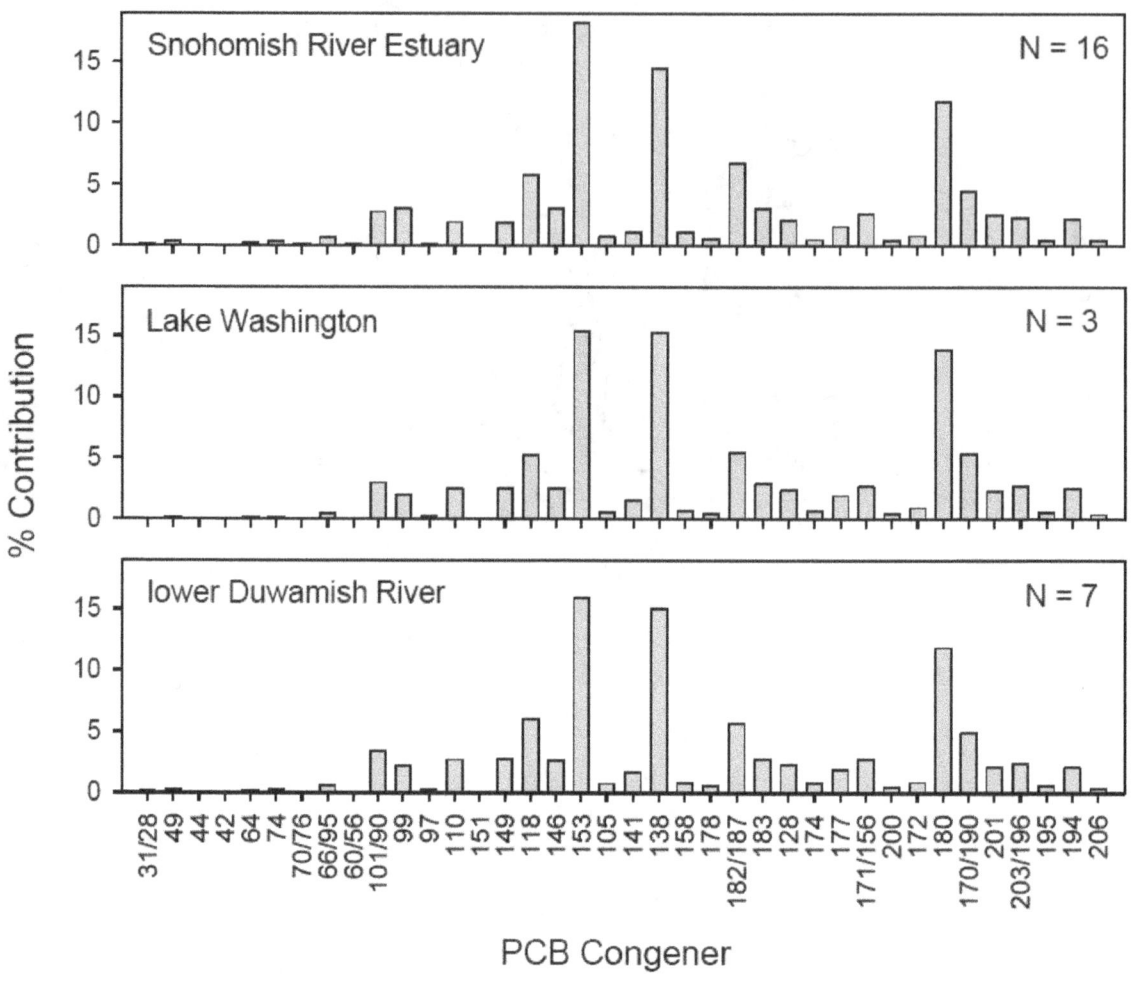

Figure 6. Percent contribution of polychlorinated biphenyl (PCB) congeners observed in osprey eggs collected from three areas in the Puget Sound, Washington in 2002–03.

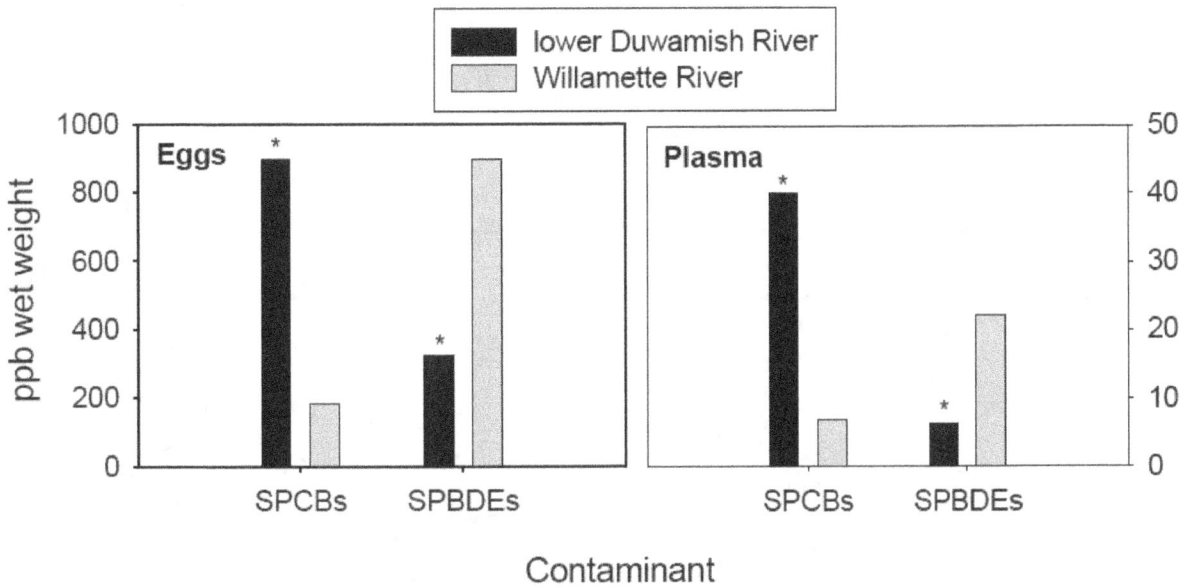

Figure 7.   Geometric mean sum of polychlorinated biphenyl (SPCBs) and sum of polybrominated diphenyl ether (SPBDEs) concentrations in osprey eggs and nestling plasma from the lower Duwamish River (LDR), Washington (2006–07) and Willamette River (WR), Oregon (2006). N eggs: LDR = 11, WR = 10; N plasma: LDR = 7, WR = 6. Asterisks indicate significant differences between rivers ($\alpha = 0.05$).

47

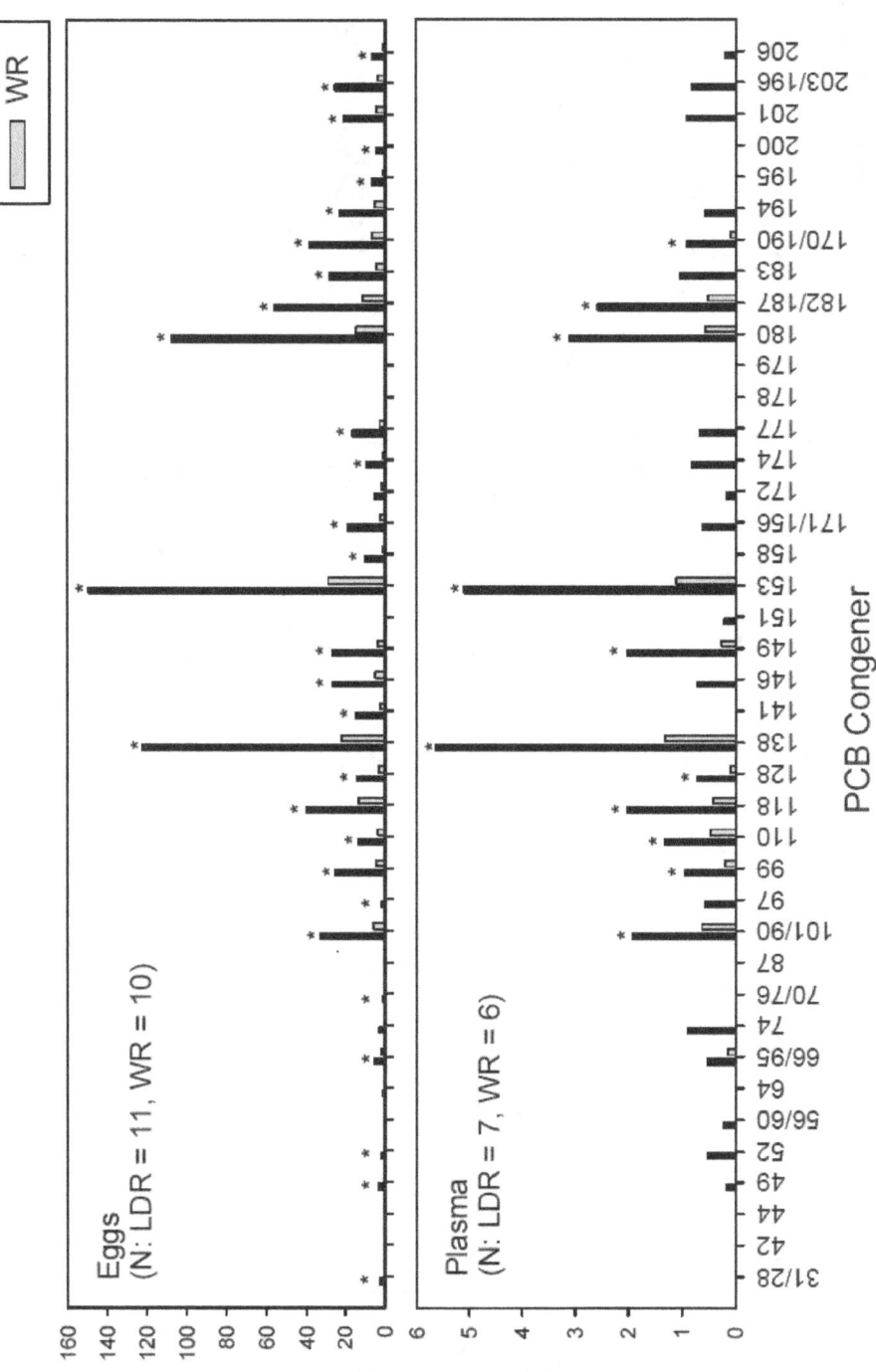

Figure 8. Geometric mean polychlorinated biphenyl (PCB) congener concentrations in osprey eggs and nestling plasma from the lower Duwamish River (LDR), Washington (2006–07) and the Willamette River (WR), Oregon (2006). Asterisks indicate significant differences between rivers (α = 0.05).

48

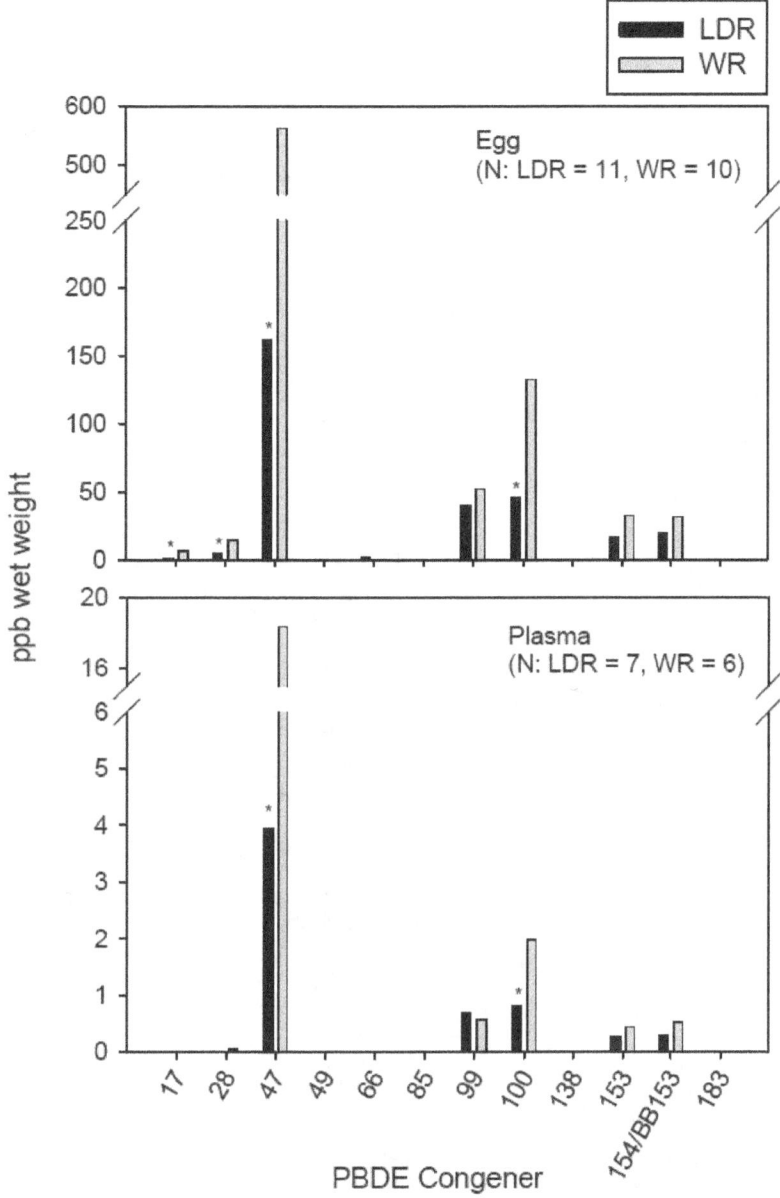

Figure 9. Geometric mean polybrominated diphenyl ether (PBDE) congener concentrations in osprey eggs and nestling plasma from the lower Duwamish River (LDR), Washington (2006–07) and the Willamette River (WR), Oregon (2006). Asterisks indicate significant differences between rivers (α = 0.05).

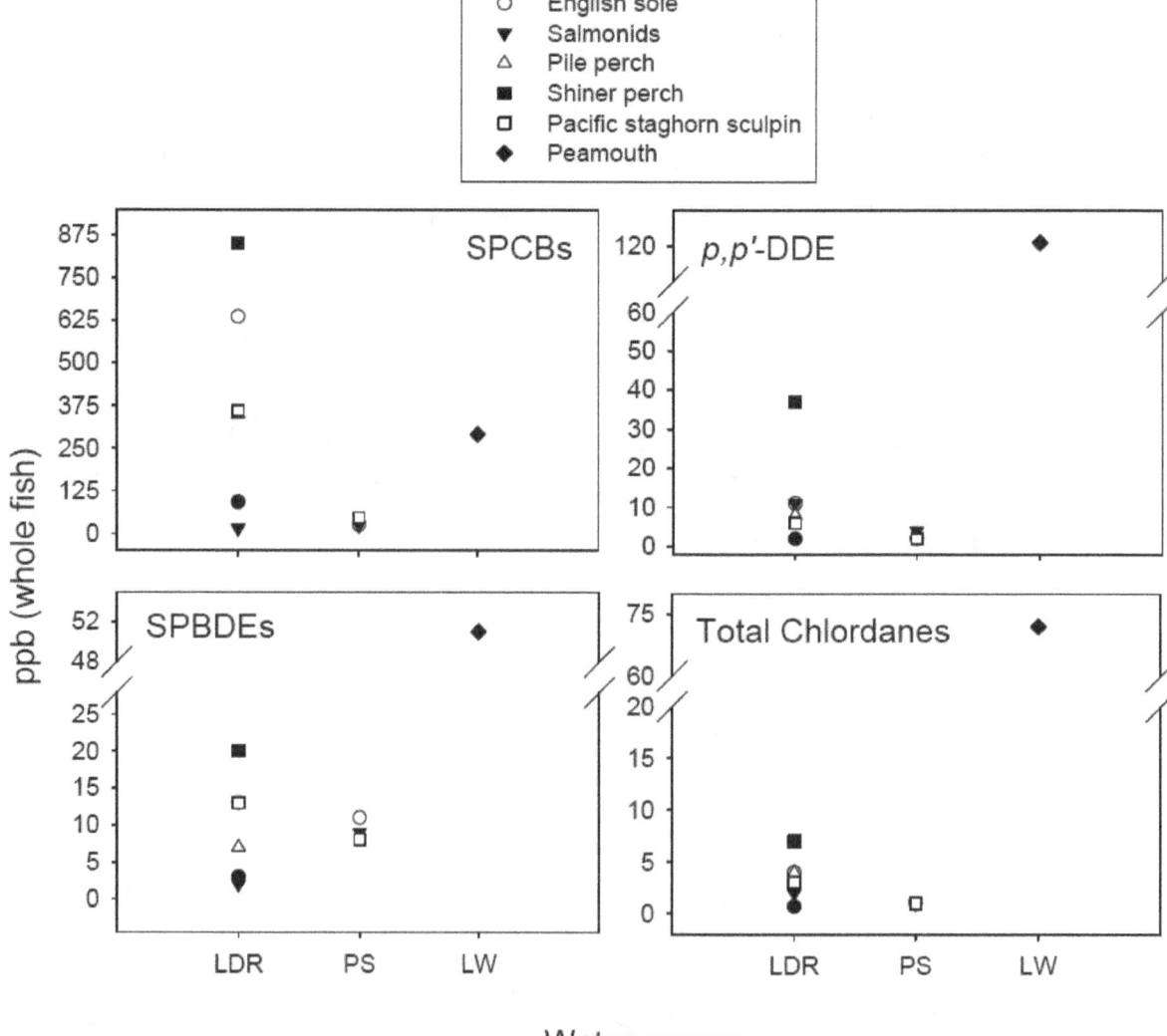

Figure 10. Sum of polychlorinated biphenyl (SPCBs), sum of polybrominated diphenyl ether (SPBDEs), *p,p'*-DDE, and total chlordane (sum of *trans*-nonachlor, *cis*-nonachlor, oxychlordane, *trans*-chlordane, *cis*-chlordane) residues in fish composites (C) from the lower Duwamish River (LDR) (Starry flounder [N=3, 1C], English sole [N=7, 1C], salmonids [age 1 year] [geo. means of steelhead (N=7, 1C), Chinook (N=7, 1C), and coho (N=7, 1C)], pile perch [N=2, 1C], shiner perch [N=7, 1C], Pacific staghorn sculpin [N=7, 1C]); Puget Sound (PS) (English sole [N=7, 1C], salmonids [age 2-3+ year] [N=2, 1C], and Pacific staghorn sculpin [N=4, 1C]); and Lake Washington (LW) (peamouth [N=7, 1C]) in 2007.

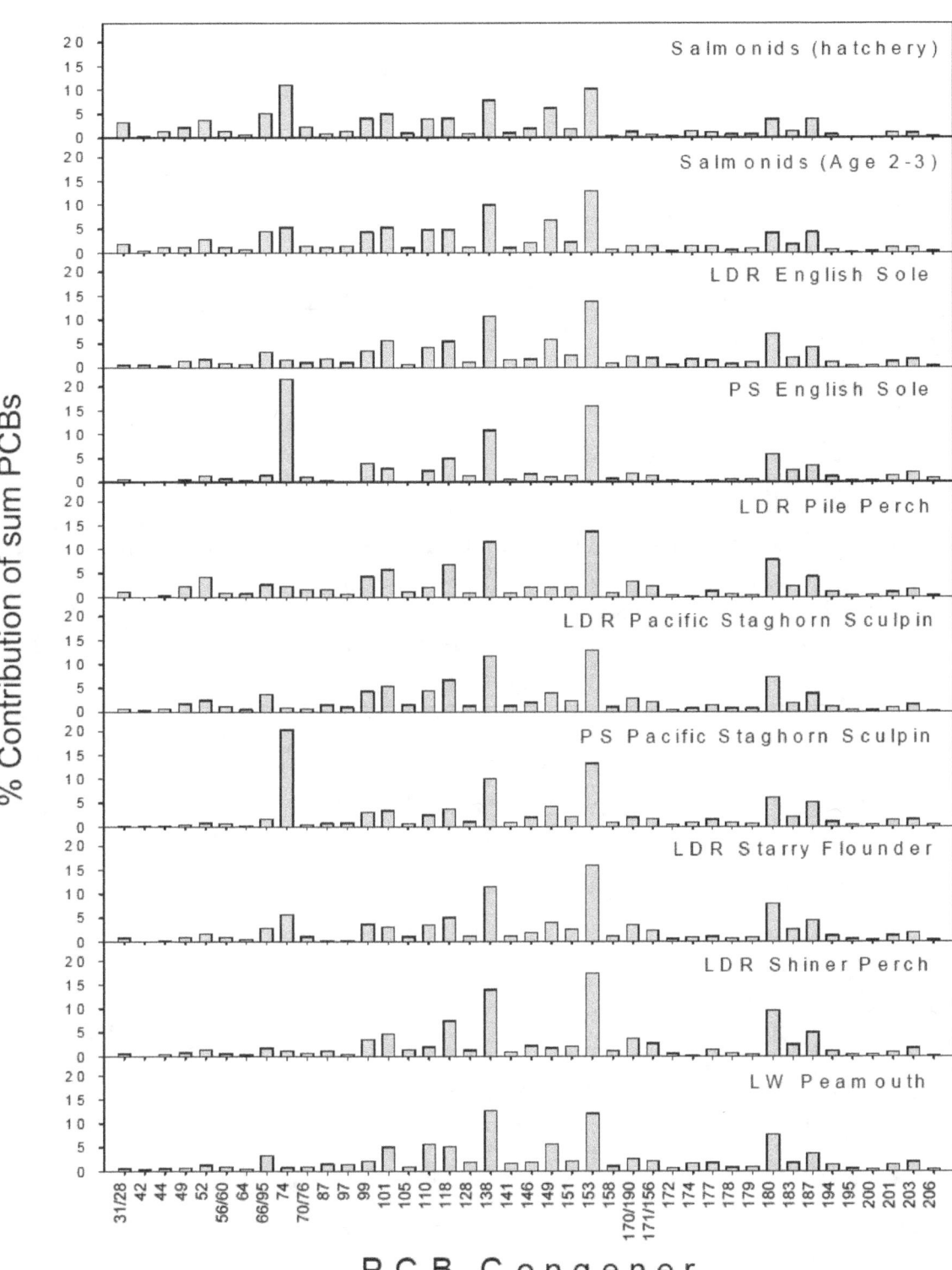

Figure 11. Percent contribution of polychlorinated biphenyl (PCB) congeners observed in fish composites from the lower Duwamish River (LDR), Puget Sound (PS), and Lake Washington (LW), Washington in 2007.

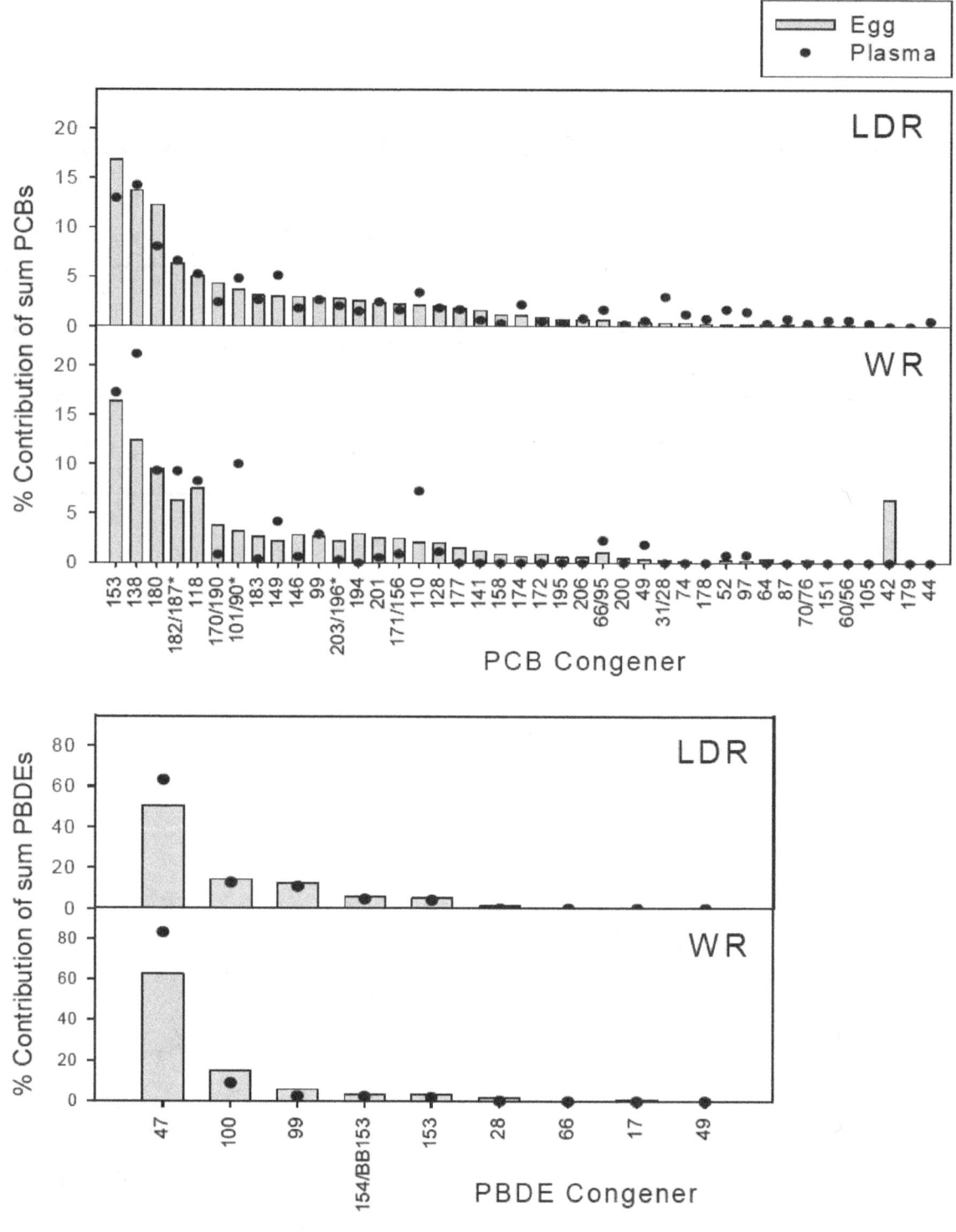

Figure 12. Polychlorinated biphenyl (PCB) and polybrominated diphenyl ether (PBDE) congener contributions observed in osprey eggs and nestling plasma from the lower Duwamish River (LDR), Washington (2006–07) (N: eggs = 11, plasma = 7) and the Willamette River (WR), Oregon (2006) (N: eggs = 10, plasma = 6). Asterisks indicate congeners that co-eluted in osprey eggs but not in plasma (plasma represents PCB congeners 187, 101, and 203 only).

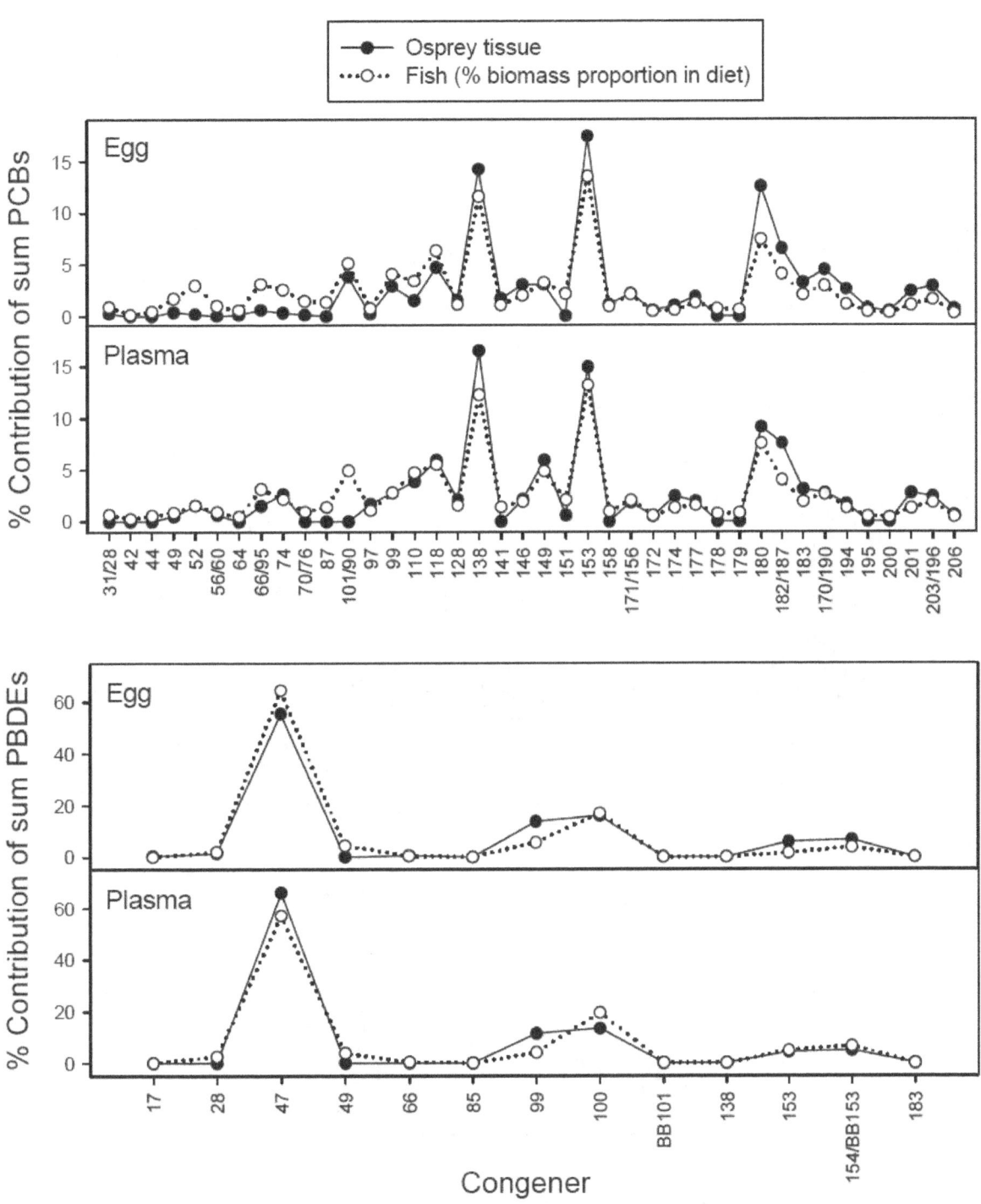

Figure 13. Polychlorinated biphenyl (PCB) and polybrominated diphenyl ether (PBDE) congener contributions observed in osprey eggs (N=11, geometric means) and nestling plasma (N=7, geometric means) from the lower Duwamish River and in fish species (calculated from percent biomass proportions observed for each respective nesting period) from areas in the Puget Sound, Washington, 2006–07.

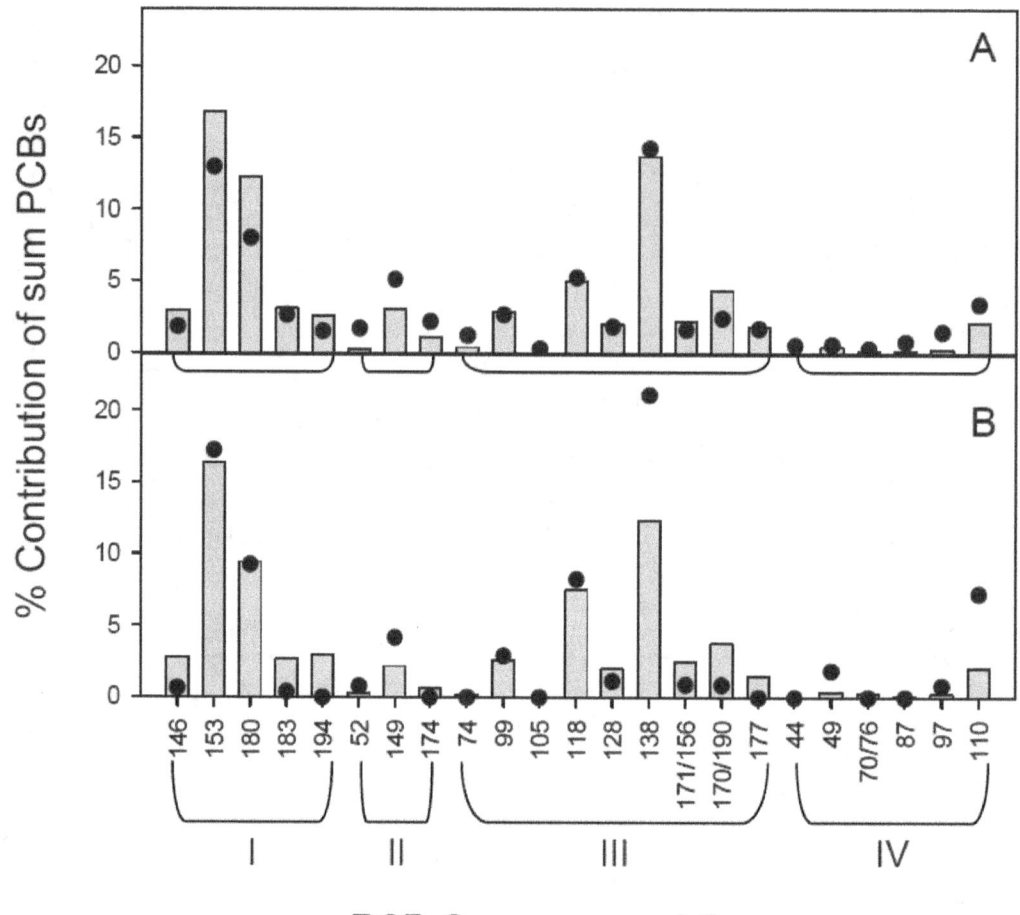

	Mean proportion			
	I	II	III	IV
LDR Egg	7.5	1.5	3.6	0.5
LDR Plasma	5.4	3.0	3.5	1.2
WR Egg	6.8	1.0	3.6	0.5
WR Plasma	5.5	1.7	3.9	1.7

Figure 14. PCB congener contributions observed in osprey eggs (bars) and plasma (dots) in the lower Duwamish River (A) and the Willamette River (B) for each metabolic group (group I, no vicinal H-atoms [e.g., *meta-para (m,p)*, *ortho-meta (o,m)*, which can be used to indicate the propensity of a congener to be metabolized, see Kannan and others, 1995]; group II, *m,p* vicinal H-atoms; group III, o,m vicinal H-atoms; group IV, both *m,p* and *o,m* vicinal H-atoms).

Table 1. Summary of whole body fish composites collected and analyzed for contaminants.

Composite ID[1]	Species	N[2]	Collection Date	Collection Site	Total Length[3]	Weight[4]
LW-PM	Peamouth	7	5/31/2007	Lake Washington	303.1 (11.9) 13.7	235.8 39.0
LDR-ES	English Sole	7	5/18/2007	LDR	261 (10.3) 14.8	147.2 22.2
LDR-PSS	Pacific Staghorn Sculpin	7	5/18/2007	LDR	163.6 (6.4) 11.9	56.9 11.7
LDR-SP	Shiner Perch	7	5/18/2007	LDR	125.1 (4.9) 5.5	24.1 3.9
LDR-SF	Starry Flounder	3	5/18/2007	LDR	229 (9.0) 27.2	123.9 49.7
LDR-PP	Pile Perch	2	5/18/2007	LDR	201.5 (7.9) 21.9	96.6 33.4
SCH-ST	Steelhead	7	4/13/2007	Soos Creek Hatchery	214.3 (8.4) 10.9	88.1 11.5
SCH-CH	Chinook	7	4/19/2007	Soos Creek Hatchery	194.1 (7.6) 9.8	69.6 9.1
SCH-CO	Coho	7	4/19/2007	Soos Creek Hatchery	148.7 (5.9) 4.4	35.0 2.3
PS-ES	English Sole	7	9/12/2007	Puget Sound[5]	258.4 (10.2) 20.1	219.9 63.9
PS-PSS	Pacific Staghorn Sculpin	4	7/3/2007	Puget Sound[e]	217.8 (8.6) 19	138.2 32.4
PS-CH	Chinook Salmon (Ad-clipped; age:2)	2	9/7/2007	Puget Sound[e]	304.0 (12.0) 0.57	324 1.41

[1]N = 1; LW = Lake Washington, LDR = lower Duwamish River, SCH = Soos Creek Hatchery, PS = Puget Sound, PM = peamouth, ES = English sole, PSS = Pacific staghorn sculpin, SP = shiner perch, SF = starry flounder, PP = pile perch, ST = steelhead, CH = chinook, CO = coho.

[2]N fish in composite sample.

[3]Arithmetic mean total length in mm (inches) followed by standard deviation (SD) in mm.

[4]Aritmetic mean mass (grams) followed by SD.

[5]Alki Point / Lowman Beach Park.

Table 2a. Percent incidence of fish families comprising the diet of ospreys for individual nests along the lower Duwamish River, Washington, during the pre-incubation and nestling periods, 2006–07.

Nesting period; NestID[6]	Fish family and category (common name)							N	Capture location[5]			
	Cyprinidae[1] (carps and minnows)	Embiotocidae (surfperches)	Ictaluridae (NA catfishes)	Pleuronectidae[2] (righteye flounders)	Salmonidae (salmon, trout)	OTHER[3]	UNK[4]		LDR	LW	PS	UNK
Pre-Incubation[6]												
T5	4.1		2.0	8.2	65.3	4.1	16.3	49	67.3	2.0	14.0	16.3
T18	21.1	5.3	5.3	2.6	52.6		13.2	38	26.3	26.3	13.2	34.2
T104		33.3		6.7	46.7		13.3	15	46.7		13.3	40.0
T105	8.3	12.5	8.3	4.2	58.3		8.3	24	58.3	20.8	4.2	16.7
CSG	5.6			5.6	66.7		22.2	18	83.3	11.1	4.2	
T115		6.7			80.0	10.0	3.3	30	96.7			3.3
HC			4.8	19.0	57.0	9.5	9.5	21	76.2	4.8		19.0
BDC		5.6	5.6	11.1	61.1	5.6	11.1	18	77.8	5.6	5.6	11.1
% Incidence	4.9	7.9	3.3	7.2	61.0	3.7	12.2		66.6	8.8	7.0	17.6
% Incidence[7]	5.6	9.0	3.7	8.2	69.3	4.2						
Mass (g)[8]	172.7	169.7	297.2	110.8	96.9	130.1						
BIOMASS	8.2	13.0	9.4	7.7	57.1	4.6						
Nestling												
T5[9]								0				
T18	37.0	6.1	3.0	21.2	60.6		9.1	33	15.2		45.4	39.4
T104		14.8		29.6	11.1	3.7	3.7	27	22.2	33.3	14.8	29.6
T105[9]								0				
CSG	14.6		19.5	39.0	7.3	7.3	12.2	41	12.2	31.7	43.9	12.2
T115	16.0	10.0	10.0	38.0	18.0	2.0	6.0	50	12.0	28.0	40.0	20.0
HC	17.9	12.8	7.7	30.8	2.6	7.7	20.5	39	30.8	23.1	38.5	7.7
BDC	16.7	8.3	12.5	29.2	20.8	8.3	4.2	24	16.7	33.3	41.7	8.3
CMP	48.6			25.7	5.7		20.0	35	5.7	51.4	20.0	22.9
% Incidence	21.5	7.4	7.5	30.5	18.0	4.1	10.8		16.4	28.7	34.9	20.0
% Incidence[7]	24.1	8.3	8.4	34.2	20.2	4.6						
Mass (g)[8]	146.4	53.5	235.1	149.6	310.9	200.0						
BIOMASS	19.3	2.4	10.8	28.0	34.4	5.0						

[1] Predominantly peamouth (98.6%) with respect to the entire nesting period (N = 72).

[2] Predominantly soles (83.3%) with respect to the entire nesting period (N = 108); see table 2b for additional breakdown during the pre-incubation period.

[3] Other = Clupeidae (herring) (N=1), Cottidae (sculpins) (N=1), Osmeridae (smelts) N=9, Percidae (perches) N=5, Chimaeridae (ratfish) N=1, and Catostomidae (largescale sucker) N=1; pre-incubation other category included only sculpins (N=3) and smelts (N=4).

[4] Unknown.

[5] LDR = lower Duwamish River, LW = Lake Washington, PS = Puget Sound (includes Elliott Bay), UNK = unknown.

[6] CMP not included in summary calculation due to small sample size (N=5).

[7] Percent incidence when unknown fish are assumed to be found in same proportions observed in the diet.

[8] Mass determined by calculating means of fish (relative to species contributions) length (converted to mass) for each respective osprey nesting period.

[9] Nest failed to produce young in 2006 and 2007.

Table 2b. Further breakdown of fish species (% incidence) captured by osprey nesting along the lower Duwamish River in 2006–07 during the pre-incubation period with corresponding fish weights and percent biomass.

NestID[4]	N	Cyprinidae[2] carps, minnows	Embiotocidae pile perch	Embiotocidae shiner perch	Ictaluridae NA catfishes	Pleuronectidae SF-LDR	Pleuronectidae SF-PS	Pleuronectidae ES-PS	Salmonidae Age 1 Year	Salmonidae Age 2-3+ Year	Other[3] sculpin	Other[3] smelts	Unknown
T5	49	4.1			2.0			8.2	65.3			4.1	16.3
T18	38	21.1	5.3		5.3			2.6	44.7	7.9			13.2
T104	15		33.3					6.7	33.3	13.3			13.3
T105	24	8.3	12.5		8.3	4.2			54.2	4.2			8.3
CSG	18	5.6						5.6	66.7				22.2
T115	30		6.7						80.0		10.0		3.3
HC	21				4.8	14.3	4.8		57.1			9.5	9.5
BDC	18			5.6	5.6	5.6	5.6		61.1		5.6		11.1
% Incidence		4.9	7.2	0.7	3.3	3.0	1.3	2.9	57.8	3.2	2.0	1.7	12.2
% Incidence[5]		5.56	8.23	0.79	3.70	3.41	1.48	3.29	65.76	3.62	2.22	1.93	
Mass (g)		172.7	183.8	25.8	297.2	110.8	110.8	110.8	88.9	240.9	70.5	200.0	
BIOMASS (%)		8.16	12.86	0.17	9.35	3.22	1.39	3.10	49.73	7.41	1.33	3.29	

[1]PS = Puget Sound including Elliott Bay, SF = starry flounder, LDR = lower Duwamish River, ES = English sole.
[2]Predominantly peamouth (98.6%).
[3]Captured by osprey in the PS.
[4]CMP not included in summary because of low sample size (N=5, salmonids caught in the LDR) during the pre-incubation period.
[5]Percent incidence when unknown fish are assumed to be found in same proportions observed in the diet.

57

Table 3. Osprey nest and egg characteristics along the lower Duwamish River, Washington and Willamette River, Oregon, 2006–07.

[D = lower Duwamish River, W = Willamette River, Adj Fac = adjustment factor, Dev = development, NA = not applicable]

River-NestID[1]	Collection Date	Clutch Size[2]	Whole Egg Weight (g)	Egg Contents Weight (g)	Adj Fac	Volume (mL)	Dev (days)	Initiation Date (julian date)[3]
D-T5	6/08/06	0	NA	NA	NA	NA	NA	5/31/06 (151)
D-T18	6/08/06	1-1[4]	73.26	65.98	0.895	73.7	4	5/30/06 (150)
D-T104	6/08/06	3-1	62.16	52.72	0.848	62.2	6	5/08/06 (128)
D-T105	6/08/06	0	NA	NA	NA	NA	NA	5/11/06 (131)
D-CSG	5/25/06	3-1	69.98	59.27	0.884	68.2	7	5/18/06 (138)
D-T115	6/08/06	3-1	62.60	53.49	0.832	64.3	7	6/01/06 (152)
D-HC	5/25/06	3-1	67.06	57.71	0.786	73.4	17	5/08/06 (128)
D-BDC	6/01/06	3-1	71.62	62.79	0.877	71.6	12	5/20/06 (140)
D-CMP	5/25/06	3-1	53.96	45.74	0.791	57.8	22	5/03/06 (123)
D-T5	5/25/07	1	NA	NA	NA	NA	NA	5/20/07 (140)
D-T18	5/25/07	3-1[5]	66.63	57.23	0.919	62.3	0-4	5/21/07 (141)
D-T104	5/25/07	3-1	65.02	55.00	0.795	69.2	23	5/02/07 (122)
D-T105	5/25/07	2-1	58.44	49.61	0.819	60.6	21	5/04/07 (124)
D-CMP	7/11/07	4[7]	48.67	40.57	0.749	54.2	38	4/19/07 (109)
W-15B	5/17/06	4-1	71.37	62.55	0.859	72.8	17	4/30/06 (120)
W-21	5/17/06	3-1	76.73	67.24	0.880	76.4	17	4/30/06 (120)
W-30C	5/17/06	3-1	59.31	50.93	0.824	61.8	21	4/26/06 (116)
W-60	5/18/06	3-1	69.87	61.41	0.858	71.6	23	4/25/06 (115)
W-79B	5/18/06	2+1-1[8]	64.11	55.97	0.793	70.6	36	4/12/06 (102)
W-97D	5/18/06	3-1	66.83	58.85	0.841	70.0	25	4/23/06 (113)
W-99A	5/18/06	4-1	76.64	67.90	0.866	78.4	12	5/06/06 (126)
W-111	5/19/06	3-1	68.53	59.32	0.843	70.4	25	4/24/06 (114)
W-122	5/19/06	3-1	59.54	52.00	0.818	63.6	37	4/12/06 (102)
W-132A	5/19/06	3-1	63.44	55.59	0.830	67.0	21	4/28/06 (118)
D mean		2.3	63.6	54.6		65.2	15.3	5/18/06 (138)
W mean		3.2	67.6	59.2		70.3	23.4	4/25/06 (115)
P-value		0.0464	0.1971	0.1283		0.0655	0.0772	<0.0001[9]

[1]No eggs were present at T5 (2006 and 2007) and T105 (2006) nests on day of collection in 2006; T5 nest had one egg on day of collection in 2007 and thus was not collected. No more eggs were laid and this nest failed by 6/18/07.

[2]Clutch size minus egg collected.

[3]Initiation date estimated by back-calculation from days of development (actual date ± 3 days of estimated date); when days of development was not available initiation date was based on visual observation.

[4]Egg was cold when collected.

[5]Clutch size was two on day of collection (2-1), female laid third egg after sampling date.

[6]Development of egg could not be determined; egg was black and rotten at collection.

[7]Two addled eggs were collected on day of blood sampling (7/11/07), only one was measured and analyzed.

[8]2 eggs + 1 nestling – 1 egg.

[9]Statistical test used julian date and only included 2006 data.

Table 4. A summary of nesting success for ospreys along the lower Duwamish River (LDR), Washington and the Willamette River (WR), Oregon.

Reproductive Parameter	LDR[1] 2003	LDR 2006	WR[2] 2006	LDR 2007	WR[2] 2007
Total nests found	12	9	10[3]	9	10[3]
Occupied nests[4]	12	9	10	9	10
Active nests[4]	11	9	10	9	10
% Active	92	100	100	100	100
Successful nests	8	5	9	7	10
% Successful (occupied)	66.7	55.6	90.0	77.8	100
% Successful (active)	72.7	55.6	90.0	77.8	100
No. advanced age nestlings	17	10	15	15	22
Productivity (occupied, w/ 1 egg collected)	1.42	1.43	1.50	1.50	NA[5]
Productivity (occupied, w/o egg collected)	NA[6]	0.00[7]	NA[6]	1.80	2.20
Productivity (occupied, combined)	1.42	1.11	1.50	1.67	2.20
Productivity (active, all active nests had 1 egg collected)	1.55	1.11	1.50	1.67	2.20

[1]Includes nests from the LDR (N = 7), Lake Washington (N = 3) and Elliott Bay (N = 1, not included in residue analysis).

[2]The reference site; 10 nests were randomly chosen for monitoring from a nesting population of >200 pairs.

[3]Total population was not surveyed on the WR in 2006 or 2007; total nests found represents nests chosen and monitored for study purposes and does not reflect total number of nests present along the WR during 2006 and 2007.

[4]Active and occupied nests follow the definitions of Postupalsky (1974, 1977).

[5]Not applicable, no eggs were collected from the reference site in 2007.

[6]Not applicable; all nests that contained eggs had one egg collected.

[7]Two nests failed prior to egg collection despite observed incubating behavior several weeks prior and subsequent to day of collection (6/8/06).

Table 5. Geometric mean contaminant concentrations (ranges) and Toxic Equivalent concentrations (TEQs) in osprey eggs from three areas of the Puget Sound, Washington, 2002–03.

[NC = not calculated, that is, <50% of samples contained detectable residues; number of samples with detectable residues identified in [ ]; ND = not detected (less than detection limit); ww = wet weight, dw = dry weight. Means sharing the same letter do not differ among locations]

Contaminant[1]	Snohomish River Estuary (N=16)[2]	Lake Washington (N=3)	lower Duwamish River (N=7)	P-Value[3]
OCs (µg/kg ww)				
QCB	0.33 (ND-2.03)	0.45 (0.19-0.89)	0.32 (0.18-0.64)	0.8630
HCB	3.07 (1.01-19.4)	2.35 (1.30-4.67)	2.08 (1.19-4.55)	0.4785
OCS	0.22 (ND-2.47)	4.76 (0.14-0.39)	0.32 (0.16-0.89)	0.6465
Mirex	2.23 (1.41-3.94) B	6.01 (4.48-8.12) A	3.77 (1.41-10.0) AB	0.0024
β-HCH	1.46 (0.66-3.18)	0.75 (0.21-1.46)	1.65 (1.05-3.68)	0.1280
Total Chlordanes	5.92 (2.81-12.8) B	30.4 (33.7-54.5) A	34.5 (21.8-96.2) A	<0.0001
DDD	11.7 (2.39-96.2) B	42.9 (19.6-64.8) AB	142 (20.9-278) A	<0.0001
DDE	601 (155-1110) B	939 (843-1,090) AB	1,197 (937-1,400) A	0.0082
DDT	0.68 (ND-3.06) B	4.07 (1.82-10.1) A	10.3 (0.98-52.0) A	<0.0001
HE	2.01 (1.19-4.06) B	9.31 (7.23-14.6) A	7.77 (4.48-16.4) A	<0.0001
Dieldrin	1.13 (0.22-4.32) B	4.16 (1.39-3.73) A	2.83 (1.06-9.54) AB	0.0100
PCBs (µg/kg ww)				
Sum Congeners	742 (477-1410) B	2633 (2360-3,230) A	1914 (769-3,670) A	<0.0001
Coplanar PCBs (ng/kg ww)				
77	38.7 (ND-348) B	583 (162-825) A	254 (41.5-945) AB	0.0193
81	5.71 (ND-187) B	576 (432-884) A	3.28 (ND-358) B	0.0220
126	201 (117-611) B	1,133 (1083-1,296) A	889 (287-2,245) A	<0.0001
169	19.0 (7.93-90.1) B	138 (129-149) A	93.1 (28.6-254) A	<0.0001
Dioxins and Furans[4] (ng/kg ww)				
2378 TCDD	1.01 (ND-3.83)	2.85 (2.07-3.76)	2.61 (1.79-5.08)	0.1030
Total TCDD	1.01 (ND-3.83)	2.85 (2.07-3.76)	2.61 (1.60-5.08)	0.1030
12378 P5CDD	2.43 (ND-42.5) B	14.2 (11.5-16.2) A	12.08 (ND-25.1) A	0.0346
Total P5CDD	2.43 (ND-42.5)	14.2 (11.5-16.2)	5.40 (ND-25.1)	0.2695
123478 H6CDD	0.22 (ND-2.25) B	3.32 (2.58-4.85) A	3.46 (1.36-7.43) A	0.0010
123678 H6CDD	6.32 (ND-263)	22.3 (13.7-44.2)	21.16 (9.46-44.4)	0.1592
123789 H6CDD	1.05 (ND-124)	3.44 (2.09-6.51)	4.64 (1.30-12.4)	0.1808
Total H6CDD	8.19 (ND-461)	29.5 (19.3-55.6)	30.1 (12.1-64.3)	0.1582
1234678 H7CDD	8.69 (ND-2,160)	70.95 (24.4-266)	47.13 (7.52-154)	0.1361
Total H7CDD	8.75 (ND-2,160)	73.9 (54.9-266)	48.7 (7.52-154)	0.1298
OCDD	35.0 (3.83-1,550)	376 (144-2,110)	125 (10.5-1,040)	0.1212
2378 TCDF	NC [7] (ND-0.88)	NC [1] (ND-0.73)	NC [3] (ND-0.38)	-
Total TCDF	NC [7] (ND-0.88)	NC [1] (ND-0.73)	NC [3] (ND-0.52)	-
12378 P5CDF	ND	ND	ND	-
23478 P5CDF	0.95 (ND-12.9)	1.37 (ND-8.23)	3.16 (ND-14.79)	0.3814

Table 5. Geometric mean contaminant concentrations (ranges) and Toxic Equivalent concentrations (TEQs) in osprey eggs from three Puget Sound areas, Washington, 2002–03.—Continued

Contaminant[1]	Snohomish River Estuary (N=16)[2]	Lake Washington (N=3)	lower Duwamish River (N=7)	P-Value[3]
Dioxins and Furans[4] (ng/kg ww)				
Total P5CDF	0.95 (ND-12.9)	8.05 (6.19-10.2)	3.48 (ND-17.1)	0.0772
123478 H6CDF	0.24 (ND-22.9)	0.39 (ND-1.22)	0.40 (ND-2.92)	0.8172
234678 H6CDF	0.20 (ND-16.6)	0.99 (0.77-1.59)	0.62 (ND-1.78)	0.1429
123678 H6CDF	0.26 (ND-29.6) B	1.34 (1.03-1.96) A	1.51 (0.44-3.37) A	0.0333
Total H6CDF	0.66 (ND-72.1) B	3.73 (3.20-4.57) A	5.02 (0.79-11.0) A	0.0353
1234678 H7CDF	NC [1] (ND-24.65)	5.41 (2.51-13.7)	0.90 (ND-17.4)	-
1234789 H7CDF	NC [2] (ND-2.75)	0.19 (ND-1.06)	NC [2] (ND-1.61)	-
Total H7CDF	NC [2] (ND-31.9)	10.0 (4.63-27.4)	5.40 (1.57-25.5)	0.6888
OCDF	NC [3] (ND-6.08)	1.60 (4.63-27.4)	0.36 (1.57-25.5)	0.1838
PBDEs (µg/kg ww)				
Sum Congeners	242 (124-384)	242 (121-439)	214 (197-365)	0.7386
Pesticides[5] (ng/kg ww)				
Dacthal	0.68 (ND-10.3)	NC [1] (ND-6.49)	NC [2] (ND-5.09)	-
Di-TCP	22.7 (9.64-85.5)	8.50 (7.68-9.56)	12.0 (7.66-19.0)	0.1065
Metals				
Hg (mg/kg dw)	0.46[6] (0.15-1.21)	0.48 (0.25-0.71)	0.72 (0.26-1.7)	0.5968
TEQs[7] (ng/kg ww)	43 (20-109) B	231 (193-283) A	161 (92-305) A	<0.0001

[1]OCs=organochlorine pesticides, QCB=pentachlorobenzene, HCB=hexachlorobenzene, OCS=octachlorostyrene, β-HCH=beta-hexachlorocyclohexane, total Chlordanes=sum of oxychlordane, *trans*-chlordane, *cis*-chlordane, *trans*-nonachlor, *cis*-nonachlor, DDD=*p,p*'-DDD, DDE=*p,p*'-DDE, DDT= *p,p*'-DDT, HE=heptachlor epoxide, PCBs=polychlorinated biphenyls, TCDD=tetrachlorodibenzo-*p*-dioxin, P5CDD=pentachlorodibenzo-*p*-dioxin, H6CDD=hexachlorodibenzo-*p*-dioxin, H7CDD=heptachlorodibenzo-*p*-dioxin, OCDD=octachlorodibenzo-*p*-dioxin, TCDF=tetrachlorodibenzofuran, P5CDF=pentachlorodibenzofuran, H6CDF=hexachlorodibenzofuran, H7CDF=heptachlorodibenzofuran, OCDF=octachlorodibenzofuran, PBDEs=polybrominated diphenyl ethers, Di-TCP=dimethyl-TCP, Hg=total mercury.

[2]N = 15 for dioxins, furans, TEQs.

[3]Tukey's Standardized Range Test (α = 0.05) was used to separate means.

[4]123789H6CDF was not detected in any samples.

[5]Additional pesticides analyzed and not detected = atrazine, cyanazine, trichlopyr, simazine, alachlor, metolachlor, 24D, 24DB, 235T, MCPA, picloram, carbaryl and methomyl.

[6]N = 4; eggs sampled in 2002 not analyzed for mercury.

[7]Total Toxic Equivalents concentrations (TEQ) to sum of 2,3,7,8-TCDD following Van den Berg and others, 1998.

Table 6. Polychlorinated biphenyl (PCB) concentrations (µg/kg, wet weight) (including geometric means and comparisons) in osprey eggs from the lower Duwamish River, Washington (N = 11), and the Willamette River, Oregon (N = 10), 2006–07.

[D = lower Duwamish River, W = Willamette River, RM = river mile, ND = not detected (less than detection limit), NC = not calculated (>50% samples less than detection limit). Geometric means were calculated using one-half of the detection limit when >50% of the samples contained detectable residues]

River-NestID	RM	Total PCBs		PCB Congener											
		ΣPCB Congeners	Aroclor 1254:1260	31/28	42	44	49	52	56/60	64	66/95	74	70/76	87	101/90
D-T18	0.0	839.67	1,728.03	0.51	ND	0.14	1.84	0.85	ND	1.80	4.65	2.35	0.55	ND	31.19
D-T104	0.1	739.13	1,508.50	2.85	0.57	0.17	5.72	2.70	1.23	3.63	7.44	4.37	2.04	4.88	31.42
D-CSG	1.0	613.36	1,059.08	3.92	ND	0.12	1.59	1.71	ND	1.36	5.08	3.14	1.62	ND	19.05
D-T115	1.5	2,651.93	5,713.59	3.49	ND	0.38	7.39	4.96	2.91	5.34	16.37	11.16	3.42	12.12	81.69
D-HC	4.4	1,201.27	2,272.16	1.80	ND	0.46	3.21	2.69	2.06	3.17	9.38	5.53	1.86	ND	34.27
D-BDC	4.9	304.59	610.12	0.54	ND	ND	1.30	0.39	ND	1.05	2.87	1.68	0.46	ND	14.25
D-CMP	5.7	1,193.17	2,400.59	6.79	0.81	ND	3.50	1.45	ND	3.78	8.46	4.99	2.27	8.85	42.92
D-T18[1]	0.0	1,187.13	2,317.77	1.58	ND	0.05	4.47	3.17	1.36	0.19	5.47	2.15	0.89	ND	35.01
D-T104[1]	0.1	692.95	1,840.66	1.28	0.32	0.02	4.62	2.33	0.48	1.32	2.09	0.61	0.66	ND	34.70
D-T105[1]	0.4	600.70	1,635.16	6.71	ND	0.04	3.16	1.54	0.46	0.21	3.64	2.89	1.12	ND	25.14
D-CMP[1]	5.7	1,389.27	3,919.63	8.22	ND	0.05	4.88	2.48	0.47	0.25	4.15	2.25	1.96	ND	47.87
W-15B	61.2	108.04	215.19	ND	ND	ND	0.38	ND	ND	0.33	1.07	ND	0.32	ND	3.72
W-21	66.2	340.44	581.26	1.18	ND	0.13	1.34	0.59	ND	0.85	3.10	ND	0.69	ND	8.03
W-30C	75.2	144.18	260.40	0.15	ND	0.16	0.75	0.53	ND	0.93	2.06	ND	0.49	ND	5.30
W-60	105	60.28	118.35	ND	ND	ND	0.33	ND	ND	0.26	0.84	ND	ND	ND	2.57
W-79B	120	723.56	433.91	ND	460.05	ND	1.09	ND	ND	ND	2.76	2.32	0.79	4.93	10.69
W-97D	135	83.76	159.87	0.61	ND	0.11	0.46	0.54	ND	0.46	1.39	0.69	0.38	ND	3.94
W-99A	138	112.05	183.36	0.25	ND	ND	0.26	0.09	ND	0.22	0.99	ND	0.32	ND	3.48
W-111	146	458.40	671.91	2.37	0.57	0.09	2.04	3.24	ND	2.71	4.89	2.96	1.84	ND	12.97
W-122	152	192.43	339.77	0.77	ND	ND	0.39	0.36	ND	0.65	1.26	ND	0.34	ND	4.87
W-132A	157	207.51	443.50	0.78	ND	ND	0.68	0.51	ND	0.78	1.99	ND	0.47	ND	7.84
Duwamish mean		897.02	1,936.40	2.39	NC	0.08	3.34	1.85	0.24	1.21	5.40	2.94	1.28	NC	32.77
Willamette mean		181.94	294.84	0.22	NC	NC	0.62	0.19	ND	0.43	1.75	NC	0.38	NC	5.59
P-value[2]		<0.0001	<0.0001	0.0013	-	-	<0.0001	0.0010	-	0.0726	0.0003	-	0.0074	-	<0.0001

[1]Eggs collected in 2007, all others collected in 2006.
[2]Comparison between Duwamish and Willamette means.

Table 6. Polychlorinated biphenyl (PCB) concentrations (µg/kg, wet weight) (including geometric means and comparisons) in osprey eggs from the lower Duwamish River, Washington (N = 11), and the Willamette River, Oregon (N = 10), 2006–07.—Continued

River-NestID	RM	PCB Congener													
		97	99	110	118	128	138	141	146	149	151	153	158	171/156	172
D-T18	0.0	1.88	21.03	25.72	54.00	26.04	126.15	16.25	24.38	25.28	ND	123.71	11.35	12.05	11.02
D-T104	0.1	2.98	31.63	30.84	53.31	20.88	110.12	10.89	20.21	23.41	0.57	112.27	11.59	8.79	4.54
D-CSG	1.0	1.16	12.34	15.47	31.87	13.69	77.31	10.89	16.06	14.03	0.94	90.48	7.33	19.53	9.04
D-T115	1.5	4.47	74.87	63.56	169.21	84.05	417.09	42.67	72.22	46.11	2.14	391.40	30.80	88.28	23.34
D-HC	4.4	1.33	30.73	28.28	79.33	33.86	165.87	19.79	36.37	20.58	1.53	189.65	18.12	40.73	ND
D-BDC	4.9	0.92	9.92	10.57	20.75	8.27	44.54	5.06	8.51	10.85	ND	47.39	3.51	8.53	3.01
D-CMP	5.7	2.34	30.38	40.18	74.45	37.22	175.24	22.63	34.78	34.94	ND	172.29	16.27	16.40	15.80
D-T18[1]	0.0	2.34	21.85	4.74	19.98	4.36	112.80	19.34	31.86	50.18	7.41	208.17	7.83	21.90	11.73
D-T104[1]	0.1	1.37	28.17	2.87	16.83	3.97	89.58	10.09	23.31	27.63	0.80	149.99	5.42	13.13	6.37
D-T105[1]	0.4	1.85	19.24	3.49	26.03	3.68	79.58	8.62	19.95	22.44	1.05	119.00	5.78	13.29	5.04
D-CMP[1]	5.7	1.90	35.03	4.44	28.94	6.50	190.76	21.31	46.52	43.63	0.89	289.47	11.36	25.71	14.27
W-15B	61.2	0.31	2.79	2.16	9.68	2.01	15.71	1.36	3.27	2.37	ND	20.51	1.76	2.93	0.83
W-21	66.2	0.62	7.29	5.61	21.21	4.66	42.43	4.04	9.85	5.72	ND	59.31	5.08	4.13	3.35
W-30C	75.2	0.56	3.14	3.21	9.88	2.33	19.01	2.19	3.97	5.15	0.22	24.26	2.21	3.95	1.13
W-60	104.5	0.18	2.59	1.67	5.07	1.56	8.64	0.64	1.68	1.45	ND	10.25	0.85	1.42	0.40
W-79B	119.8	0.47	7.17	6.43	30.40	4.89	31.68	3.75	7.59	5.57	ND	42.82	1.45	ND	5.92
W-97D	135.3	0.28	3.35	2.54	8.43	2.32	11.67	1.13	2.33	2.04	ND	14.02	0.52	2.31	0.54
W-99A	137.9	0.29	3.09	2.32	7.96	2.73	13.39	1.19	4.09	3.05	0.19	21.29	0.51	3.57	0.99
W-111	145.9	0.89	8.87	10.79	27.19	7.21	49.05	7.14	13.23	10.17	ND	68.50	2.54	14.66	5.27
W-122	151.7	0.27	3.73	2.75	14.17	3.48	24.80	2.46	6.16	3.12	ND	35.22	1.29	6.44	2.16
W-132A	157.3	0.40	7.33	5.17	20.44	7.27	32.38	3.07	6.47	4.74	ND	38.51	1.36	7.05	1.96
Duwamish mean		1.86	24.98	13.11	40.51	13.49	121.98	14.65	26.34	26.24	0.42	149.26	9.86	18.78	5.04
Willamette mean		0.39	4.44	3.61	13.24	3.38	21.52	2.15	4.91	3.73	NC	28.55	1.40	2.44	1.57
P-value[2]		<0.0001	<0.0001	0.0036	0.0010	0.0014	<0.0001	<0.0001	<0.0001	<0.0001	-	<0.0001	<0.0001	0.0025	0.0980

[1]Eggs collected in 2007, all others collected in 2006.
[2]Comparison between Duwamish and Willamette means.

63

Table 6. Polychlorinated biphenyl (PCB) concentrations (µg/kg, wet weight) (including geometric means and comparisons) in osprey eggs from the lower Duwamish River, Washington (N = 11), and the Willamette River, Oregon (N = 10), 2006-07.—Continued

River-NestID	RM	PCB Congener													
		174	177	178	179	180	182/187	183	170/190	194	195	200	201	203/196	206
D-T18	0.0	10.04	19.80	ND	ND	92.61	48.28	24.73	38.31	23.60	5.46	5.57	19.99	22.71	5.86
D-T104	0.1	6.35	12.46	ND	ND	69.39	39.05	20.85	27.11	11.15	4.71	3.67	13.71	16.60	5.04
D-CSG	1.0	4.98	13.21	ND	ND	80.96	35.03	19.65	33.63	20.98	4.69	3.38	15.86	19.04	4.19
D-T115	1.5	14.81	53.22	ND	ND	316.83	144.01	89.48	134.13	61.91	19.52	12.33	56.93	73.61	15.71
D-HC	4.4	6.33	21.51	ND	ND	149.94	67.34	39.98	62.36	37.43	7.72	6.61	27.28	34.98	9.18
D-BDC	4.9	3.64	6.33	ND	ND	26.60	17.43	7.98	11.03	7.24	1.86	2.00	6.35	7.40	2.34
D-CMP	5.7	12.33	27.16	ND	ND	125.45	67.76	35.63	55.52	31.93	7.50	7.38	27.32	31.51	6.93
D-T18[1]	0.0	29.21	20.99	10.88	1.92	213.08	106.90	38.99	50.73	35.55	13.12	4.06	34.56	40.10	7.02
D-T104[1]	0.1	8.91	8.05	5.20	ND	85.21	49.24	23.26	21.16	15.61	5.02	3.06	15.36	19.19	5.46
D-T105[1]	0.4	6.18	9.44	4.49	0.17	72.97	42.16	17.75	23.99	11.72	4.36	2.11	12.33	14.96	3.43
D-CMP[1]	5.7	12.08	18.95	8.12	0.26	207.13	101.87	45.99	57.46	37.20	11.14	3.77	37.69	43.75	9.92
W-15B	61.2	0.67	1.76	ND	ND	11.68	7.18	2.85	4.04	2.13	0.59	0.57	2.33	2.11	0.64
W-21	66.2	1.97	6.11	ND	ND	53.14	24.80	11.99	17.53	10.26	2.41	1.60	9.59	9.69	2.17
W-30C	75.2	1.37	2.50	ND	ND	16.75	10.15	3.82	5.30	3.01	0.88	0.79	3.79	3.24	1.01
W-60	104.5	0.35	0.90	ND	ND	6.28	3.96	1.52	2.12	1.13	0.30	0.33	1.47	1.20	0.31
W-79B	119.8	1.90	2.90	ND	ND	25.01	16.31	6.82	10.17	13.14	1.21	ND	7.12	5.83	2.39
W-97D	135.3	0.50	1.20	ND	ND	5.35	5.24	1.89	2.50	2.28	0.33	0.43	2.04	1.54	0.40
W-99A	137.9	0.96	2.00	ND	ND	10.09	8.14	3.23	4.01	3.97	0.99	0.95	3.48	2.93	1.04
W-111	145.9	4.62	6.74	ND	ND	62.67	28.22	14.35	23.09	19.85	3.50	2.74	14.94	14.47	4.02
W-122	151.7	0.98	3.25	ND	ND	23.49	13.58	6.08	8.83	8.00	1.05	1.13	5.90	4.61	0.82
W-132A	157.3	1.37	3.51	ND	ND	2.67	13.64	6.24	8.74	7.97	1.16	1.42	5.54	4.90	1.16
Duwamish mean		8.85	16.14	NC	NC	107.71	56.03	27.79	38.36	22.41	6.45	4.25	20.63	24.79	6.02
Willamette mean		1.14	2.58	ND	ND	14.25	11.00	4.63	6.55	5.07	0.95	0.62	4.45	3.83	1.05
P-value[2]		<0.0001	<0.0001	-	-	<0.0001	<0.0001	<0.0001	<0.0001	0.0004	<0.0001	0.0004	<0.0001	<0.0001	<0.0001

[1]Eggs collected in 2007, all others collected in 2006.
[2]Comparison between Duwamish and Willamette means.

64

Table 7. Organochlorine contaminant concentrations (µg/kg, wet weight) (including geometric means and comparisons) in osprey eggs from the lower Duwamish River, Washington (N = 11), and the Willamette River, Oregon (N = 10), 2006–07.

[D = lower Duwamish River, W = Willamette River, RM = river mile, QCB = pentachlorobenzene, HCB = hexachlorobenzene, OCS = octachlorostyrene, β-HCH = beta-hexachlorocyclohexane, DDE = p,p'-DDE, DDD = p,p'-DDD, DDT = p,p'-DDT, HE = heptachlor epoxide, ND = not detected (less than detection limit), NC = not calculated (>50% samples less than detection limit). Geometric means were calculated using one-half of the detection limit when >50% of the samples contained detectable residues]

River-NestID	RM	Year	QCB	HCB	OCS	Mirex	β-HCH	Total chlordanes[1]	DDE	DDD	DDT	HE	Dieldrin
D-T18	0.0	2006	0.22	1.15	ND	3.09	0.74	14.06	8.91	58.20	2.87	2.68	1.89
D-T104	0.1	2006	0.16	0.81	ND	1.89	1.03	20.37	265.71	8.83	0.80	2.06	0.08
D-CSG	1.0	2006	0.25	1.79	0.10	2.26	0.45	11.06	420.42	12.61	0.16	0.96	1.17
D-T115	1.5	2006	2.35	4.08	0.53	7.80	2.26	9.56	5.52	20.04	1.55	5.61	3.47
D-HC	4.4	2006	0.23	1.87	ND	3.67	1.65	22.69	4.47	47.10	2.53	2.26	1.61
D-BDC	4.9	2006	0.30	1.63	0.06	1.02	0.82	9.95	470.63	34.18	2.41	1.01	1.65
D-CMP	5.7	2006	0.25	0.60	ND	4.00	1.21	27.12	708.81	50.12	2.16	3.97	0.80
D-T18	0.0	2007	0.22	0.87	ND	0.51	1.24	13.73	926.38	46.40	5.68	1.78	2.20
D-T104	0.1	2007	0.25	0.57	ND	0.42	1.30	8.82	210.25	7.37	2.56	2.42	0.76
D-T105	0.4	2007	0.24	0.69	ND	0.40	1.52	8.07	488.73	16.75	3.83	1.94	0.49
D-CMP	5.7	2007	0.66	1.10	ND	0.74	3.20	16.44	656.66	30.82	4.21	3.08	0.71
W-15B	61.2	2006	0.11	0.43	ND	0.43	0.16	1.89	7.47	31.08	7.73	0.59	0.92
W-21	66.2	2006	0.15	1.88	ND	0.82	0.10	3.45	648.91	4.73	1.29	0.86	1.70
W-30C	75.2	2006	0.14	0.69	ND	0.67	ND	25.43	435.69	13.94	2.54	6.60	3.11
W-60	104.5	2006	0.13	0.71	ND	0.21	ND	0.33	147.40	0.69	ND	0.56	0.61
W-79B	119.8	2006	0.05	0.17	ND	9.41	0.25	3.64	361.11	5.07	1.59	1.77	1.06
W-97D	135.3	2006	0.49	0.91	ND	0.28	0.22	2.74	137.54	3.21	2.62	0.86	4.81
W-99A	137.9	2006	0.11	0.68	ND	0.78	0.11	2.70	111.73	4.42	1.61	0.80	1.57
W-111	145.9	2006	0.28	1.22	ND	2.13	0.30	25.09	543.80	6.38	1.52	2.46	2.35
W-122	151.7	2006	0.46	0.68	ND	0.74	1.44	3.10	624.70	8.94	2.38	1.08	2.41
W-132A	157.3	2006	0.38	0.84	ND	1.59	0.21	3.72	290.63	3.80	2.38	1.11	1.31
Duwamish mean			0.32	1.15	NC	2.35	0.79	13.61	142.99	24.43	1.97	2.24	0.97
Willamette mean			0.18	0.70	ND	0.88	0.14	3.65	210.47	5.43	1.40	1.21	1.68
P-value[2]			0.1046	0.0813	-	0.0181	0.0006	0.0036	0.6227	0.0008	0.5570	0.0408	0.1590

[1]Total chlordanes = sum of *trans*-nonachlor, *cis*-nonachlor, oxychlordane, *trans*-chlordane, *cis*-chlordane.
[2]Comparison between Duwamish and Willamette means.

65

Table 8. Organochlorine contaminant concentrations (μg/kg, wet weight) (including geometric means and comparisons) in osprey eggs from the lower Duwamish River, Washington, 2003 (N = 7) and 2006–07 (N = 11).

[TCB1234 = 1,2,3,4-tetrachlorobenzene, QCB = pentachlorobenzene, HCB = hexachlorobenzene, OCS = octachlorostyrene, DDE = p,p'-DDE, DDD = p,p'-DDD, DDT = p,p'-DDT, HCH = hexachlorocyclohexane, Trans-Non = *trans*-nonachlor, Oxy-Chlor = oxychlordane, Trans-Chlor = *trans*-chlordane, Cis-Chlor = *cis*-chlordane, Cis-Non = *cis*-nonachlor, Tot Chlor = total chlordanes: sum of *trans*-nonachlor, *cis*-nonachlor, oxychlordane, *trans*-chlordane, *cis*-chlordane, HE = heptachlor epoxide, ND = not detected (less than detection limit), NC = not calculated (>50% samples less than detection limit). Geometric means were calculated using one-half of the detection limit when >50% of the samples contained detectable residues]

Year-NestID	TCB1234	QCB	HCB	OCS	DDT	DDD	DDE	Mirex	α-HCH	β-HCH	Trans-Non	Oxy-Chlor	Trans-Chlor	Cis-Chlor	Cis-Non	Tot Chlor	HE	Dieldrin
2003-T18	ND	0.38	1.49	0.18	13.10	176.95	1,268.63	2.74	ND	1.29	4.18	7.66	5.67	2.11	22.46	42.09	7.23	4.41
2003-T105	ND	0.19	1.38	0.16	17.31	233.43	1,188.67	3.01	ND	1.20	2.00	8.96	4.15	0.48	17.58	33.16	6.44	3.81
2003-T115	ND	0.25	1.47	0.48	2.27	20.88	937.46	6.07	ND	1.40	1.35	9.37	3.28	1.17	6.59	21.77	9.41	1.06
2003-LCP	ND	0.18	1.19	0.36	52.02	277.55	1,378.25	2.58	ND	1.05	1.68	8.18	3.99	0.82	7.49	22.16	4.48	1.06
2003-HC	ND	0.36	2.68	0.89	29.95	258.55	1,372.64	5.96	ND	3.68	3.10	15.30	4.49	0.48	17.16	40.53	7.47	2.16
2003-112	ND	0.64	3.90	0.21	16.02	128.68	945.30	1.41	ND	1.68	3.52	6.40	2.63	1.38	8.42	22.35	7.15	3.76
2003-TCT	ND	0.50	4.55	0.38	0.98	145.32	1,395.41	10.04	ND	2.39	3.79	23.06	7.72	1.40	60.20	96.17	16.37	9.54
2006-T18	ND	0.22	1.15	ND	2.87	58.20	8.91	3.09	ND	0.74	5.39	5.73	0.50	1.08	10.00	22.69	2.68	1.89
2006-T104	0.09	0.16	0.81	ND	0.80	8.83	265.71	1.89	ND	1.03	1.53	3.38	ND	0.31	4.72	9.95	2.06	0.08
2006-CSG	0.14	0.25	1.79	0.10	0.16	12.61	420.42	2.26	ND	0.45	3.96	3.66	0.21	0.52	2.71	11.06	0.96	1.17
2006-T115	0.74	2.35	4.08	0.53	1.55	20.04	5.52	7.80	ND	2.26	6.00	12.50	0.37	1.03	7.21	27.12	5.61	3.47
2006-HC	ND	0.23	1.87	ND	2.53	47.10	4.47	3.67	ND	1.65	2.98	6.42	0.39	0.52	3.76	14.06	2.26	1.61
2006-BDC	0.09	0.30	1.63	0.06	2.41	34.18	470.63	1.02	ND	0.82	1.99	2.92	0.29	0.25	4.11	9.56	1.01	1.65
2006-CMP	ND	0.25	0.60	ND	2.16	50.12	708.81	4.00	ND	1.21	1.93	9.41	0.35	0.33	8.35	20.37	3.97	0.80
2007-T18	ND	0.22	0.87	ND	5.68	46.40	926.38	1.24	ND	0.51	3.43	2.23	0.66	2.11	5.29	13.73	1.78	2.20
2007-T104	ND	0.25	0.57	ND	2.56	7.37	210.25	1.30	0.44	0.42	0.86	2.68	0.44	0.43	4.40	8.82	2.42	0.76
2007-T105	ND	0.24	0.69	ND	3.83	16.75	488.73	1.52	0.37	0.40	0.81	2.66	0.41	0.28	3.90	8.07	1.94	0.49
2007-CMP	ND	0.66	1.10	ND	4.21	30.82	656.66	3.20	0.13	0.74	1.43	5.77	1.56	0.61	7.05	16.44	3.08	0.71
2003	ND	0.32	2.08	0.32	10.33	141.88	1,197.33	3.77	ND	1.65	2.59	10.25	4.32	0.99	14.98	34.54	7.77	2.83
2006-07	NC	0.32	1.15	NC	1.97	24.43	142.99	2.35	NC	0.79	2.26	4.47	0.33	0.54	5.21	13.61	2.23	0.97
P-value[1]	-	0.9451	0.0489	-	0.0097	0.0003	0.0169	0.1421	-	0.0111	0.6432	0.0048	<0.0001	0.0670	0.0014	0.0007	<0.0001	0.0321

[1]P-value for between year comparisons.

66

Table 9. Polychlorinated biphenyl (PCB) concentrations (µg/kg wet weight) (including geometric means and comparisons) in osprey eggs from the lower Duwamish River (LDR), Washington, 2003 (N = 7) and 2006–07 (N = 11).

[ND = not detected (less than detection limit), NC = not calculated (>50% samples less than detection limit). Geometric means were calculated using one-half of the detection limit when >50% of the samples contained detectable residues]

Year-NestID	RM	ΣPCB Congeners	Aroclor 1254:1260	Aroclor 1260	PCB Congener											
					31/28	42	44	49	52	60/56[1]	64	66/95	74	70/76[1]	87	97
2003-T18	0.0	1,354.66	2,842.37	1,253.79	1.39	0.16	0.12	4.29	ND	4.79	2.81	8.59	3.37	0.82	0.90	7.11
2003-T105	0.4	1,395.61	2,908.65	1,540.29	0.84	ND	ND	3.13	ND	5.55	2.14	5.76	2.89	ND	0.59	4.96
2003-T115	1.2	3,223.14	6,888.36	3,993.81	3.83	0.13	0.28	7.23	ND	1.75	4.88	17.34	9.52	1.97	18.49	4.94
2003-LCP	1.5	1,524.37	3,346.70	1,624.21	1.58	ND	0.23	3.64	ND	1.01	2.67	8.77	5.08	0.89	0.50	4.02
2003-HC	4.4	3,584.69	7,307.34	4,217.31	5.77	0.28	0.29	10.21	2.55	ND	8.08	25.20	13.98	3.46	0.78	9.53
2003-112	5.7	769.48	1,516.94	650.08	3.64	0.54	0.34	4.18	ND	0.98	3.04	8.00	3.85	1.67	0.36	3.88
2003-TCT	8.5	3,671.64	7,095.89	4,765.13	1.94	0.41	0.44	4.87	ND	ND	4.48	15.67	6.10	0.96	ND	12.11
2006-T18	0.0	839.67	1,728.03	845.76	0.51	ND	0.14	1.84	0.85	ND	1.80	4.65	2.35	0.55	ND	1.88
2006-T104	0.1	739.13	1,508.50	633.70	2.85	0.57	0.17	5.72	2.70	1.23	3.63	7.44	4.37	2.04	4.88	2.98
2006-CSG	1.0	613.36	1,059.08	739.40	3.92	ND	0.12	1.59	1.71	ND	1.36	5.08	3.14	1.62	ND	1.16
2006-T115	1.2	2,651.93	5,713.59	2,893.39	3.49	ND	0.38	7.39	4.96	2.91	5.34	16.37	11.16	3.42	12.12	4.47
2006-HC	4.4	1,201.27	2,272.16	1,369.33	1.80	ND	0.46	3.21	2.69	2.06	3.17	9.38	5.53	1.86	ND	1.33
2006-BDC	4.9	304.59	610.12	242.93	0.54	ND	ND	1.30	0.39	ND	1.05	2.87	1.68	0.46	ND	0.92
2006-CMP	5.7	1,193.17	2,400.59	1,145.67	6.79	0.81	ND	3.50	1.45	ND	3.78	8.46	4.99	2.27	8.85	2.34
2007-T18	0.0	1,187.13	2,317.77	1,945.93	1.58	ND	0.05	4.47	3.17	1.36	0.19	5.47	2.15	0.89	ND	2.34
2007-T104	0.1	692.95	1,840.66	778.21	1.28	0.32	0.02	4.62	2.33	0.48	1.32	2.09	0.61	0.66	ND	1.37
2007-T105	0.4	600.70	1,635.16	666.41	6.71	ND	0.04	3.16	1.54	0.46	0.21	3.64	2.89	1.12	ND	1.85
2007-CMP	5.7	1,389.27	3,919.63	1,891.59	8.22	ND	0.05	4.88	2.48	0.47	0.25	4.15	2.25	1.96	ND	1.90
2003		1,913.92	3,949.56	2,071.46	2.25	0.16	0.21	4.96	NC	0.73	3.65	11.32	5.51	0.88	0.68	6.10
2006–07		897.02	1,936.40	983.65	2.39	NC	0.08	3.34	1.85	0.24	1.21	5.40	2.94	1.28	NC	1.86
P-value[2]		0.0157	0.0257	0.0449	0.8800	-	0.0544	0.1253	-	-	0.0364	0.0149	0.0774	-	-	<0.0001

[1]Congeners coeluted in 2006 and 2007 but not in 2003; groups (years) cannot be compared.

[2]P-value for between year comparisons.

67

Table 9. Polychlorinated biphenyl (PCB) concentrations (µg/kg wet weight) (including geometric means and comparisons) in osprey eggs from the lower Duwamish River (LDR), Washington, 2003 (N = 7) and 2006–07 (N = 11).—Continued

Year-NestID	RM	99	101/90[1]	105	110	118	128	138	141	146	149	151	153	158	171/156[1]	170/190
								PCB Congener								
2003-T18	0.0	34.09	58.28	10.93	47.53	80.37	32.45	207.49	24.43	34.51	55.58	2.23	210.27	9.17	36.21	58.62
2003-T105	0.4	24.65	47.07	8.27	34.99	83.06	30.75	212.33	25.30	39.11	41.98	0.41	236.28	11.19	41.26	69.99
2003-T115	1.2	83.52	88.84	25.51	59.10	182.95	79.66	502.85	44.77	88.46	49.89	1.33	518.18	27.42	100.37	186.61
2003-LCP	1.5	34.92	50.05	10.74	39.19	103.84	36.08	244.31	26.65	41.67	39.21	0.47	258.02	11.72	40.92	74.25
2003-HC	4.4	90.36	113.53	27.60	103.26	232.20	84.10	533.44	61.47	94.12	82.75	2.21	569.42	30.76	103.00	189.36
2003-112	5.7	24.41	35.04	9.75	29.53	51.34	15.96	110.74	11.66	19.70	31.86	1.12	119.01	9.50	17.78	28.00
2003-TCT	8.5	49.72	113.07	20.04	88.94	180.81	88.85	518.00	74.15	95.42	103.17	1.07	538.55	28.49	105.19	222.23
2006-T18	0.0	21.03	31.19	ND	25.72	54.00	26.04	126.15	16.25	24.38	25.28	ND	123.71	11.35	12.05	38.31
2006-T104	0.1	31.63	31.42	ND	30.84	53.31	20.88	110.12	10.89	20.21	23.41	0.57	112.27	11.59	8.79	27.11
2006-CSG	1.0	12.34	19.05	ND	15.47	31.87	13.69	77.31	10.89	16.06	14.03	0.94	90.48	7.33	19.53	33.63
2006-T115	1.2	74.87	81.69	ND	63.56	169.21	84.05	417.09	42.67	72.22	46.11	2.14	391.40	30.80	88.28	134.13
2006-HC	4.4	30.73	34.27	ND	28.28	79.33	33.86	165.87	19.79	36.37	20.58	1.53	189.65	18.12	40.73	62.36
2006-BDC	4.9	9.92	14.25	ND	10.57	20.75	8.27	44.54	5.06	8.51	10.85	ND	47.39	3.51	8.53	11.03
2006-CMP	5.7	30.38	42.92	ND	40.18	74.45	37.22	175.24	22.63	34.78	34.94	ND	172.29	16.27	16.40	55.52
2007-T18	0.0	21.85	35.01	1.20	4.74	19.98	4.36	112.80	19.34	31.86	50.18	7.41	208.17	7.83	21.90	50.73
2007-T104	0.1	28.17	34.70	0.25	2.87	16.83	3.97	89.58	10.09	23.31	27.63	0.80	149.99	5.42	13.13	21.16
2007-T105	0.4	19.24	25.14	0.70	3.49	26.03	3.68	79.58	8.62	19.95	22.44	1.05	119.00	5.78	13.29	23.99
2007-CMP	5.7	35.03	47.87	0.60	4.44	28.94	6.50	190.76	21.31	46.52	43.63	0.89	289.47	11.36	25.71	57.46
2003		42.93	66.05	14.48	52.12	115.45	44.43	288.32	32.61	50.86	53.42	1.06	304.45	16.05	53.05	94.44
2006—07		24.98	32.77	NC	13.11	40.51	13.49	121.98	14.65	26.34	26.24	0.42	149.26	9.86	18.78	38.36
P-value[2]		0.0548	-	-	0.0063	0.0046	0.0168	0.0085	0.0143	0.0337	0.0057	0.2769	0.0220	0.1105	-	0.0179

[1]Congeners coeluted in 2006 and 2007 but not in 2003; groups (years) cannot be compared.
[2]P-value for between year comparisons.

68

Table 9. Polychlorinated biphenyl (PCB) concentrations (µg/kg wet weight) (including geometric means and comparisons) in osprey eggs from the lower Duwamish River (LDR), Washington, 2003 (N = 7) and 2006–07 (N = 11).—Continued

Year-NestID	RM								PCB Congener						
		172	174	177	178	179	180	182/187	183	194	195	203/196[1]	200	201	206
2003-T18	0.0	10.50	17.12	28.36	11.05	ND	137.29	75.82	33.92	24.83	8.15	31.49	6.79	27.08	5.70
2003-T105	0.4	12.46	11.77	27.60	9.29	ND	168.66	81.51	39.26	29.23	8.12	34.08	6.95	28.70	5.48
2003-T115	1.2	30.56	11.45	56.52	13.53	ND	437.32	186.81	108.91	78.95	17.14	82.95	12.62	65.73	10.82
2003-LCP	1.5	12.53	10.70	28.38	9.02	ND	177.85	86.90	43.56	27.70	8.59	35.12	7.26	30.50	5.84
2003-HC	4.4	31.13	22.68	63.08	19.65	ND	461.80	193.15	106.60	76.88	21.43	92.70	15.66	70.05	12.19
2003-112	5.7	5.17	8.15	14.00	5.27	ND	71.18	43.93	18.25	13.07	4.49	16.91	3.55	16.12	3.50
2003-TCT	8.5	40.02	38.68	77.23	24.54	ND	521.78	228.69	103.49	100.89	25.43	107.58	16.16	95.53	16.95
2006-T18	0.0	11.02	10.04	19.80	ND	ND	92.61	48.28	24.73	23.60	5.46	22.71	5.57	19.99	5.86
2006-T104	0.1	4.54	6.35	12.46	ND	ND	69.39	39.05	20.85	11.15	4.71	16.60	3.67	13.71	5.04
2006-CSG	1.0	9.04	4.98	13.21	ND	ND	80.96	35.03	19.65	20.98	4.69	19.04	3.38	15.86	4.19
2006-T115	1.2	23.34	14.81	53.22	ND	ND	316.83	144.01	89.48	61.91	19.52	73.61	12.33	56.93	15.71
2006-HC	4.4	ND	6.33	21.51	ND	ND	149.94	67.34	39.98	37.43	7.72	34.98	6.61	27.28	9.18
2006-BDC	4.9	3.01	3.64	6.33	ND	ND	26.60	17.43	7.98	7.24	1.86	7.40	2.00	6.35	2.34
2006-CMP	5.7	15.80	12.33	27.16	ND	ND	125.45	67.76	35.63	31.93	7.50	31.51	7.38	27.32	6.93
2007-T18	0.0	11.73	29.21	20.99	10.88	1.92	213.08	106.90	38.99	35.55	13.12	40.10	4.06	34.56	7.02
2007-T104	0.1	6.37	8.91	8.05	5.20	ND	85.21	49.23	23.26	15.61	5.02	19.19	3.05	15.36	5.46
2007-T105	0.4	5.04	6.18	9.44	4.49	0.17	72.97	42.16	17.75	11.72	4.36	14.96	2.11	12.33	3.43
2007-CMP	5.7	14.27	12.08	18.95	8.12	0.26	207.13	101.87	45.99	37.20	11.13	43.75	3.77	37.69	9.92
2003		16.43	15.07	36.46	11.80	ND	226.82	109.98	53.61	39.90	11.32	47.27	8.74	40.15	7.57
2006–07		5.04	8.85	16.14	NC	NC	107.71	56.03	27.79	22.41	6.45	24.79	4.25	20.63	6.02
P-value[2]		0.1448	0.0685	0.0132	-	-	0.0449	0.0345	0.0543	0.1041	0.0860	-	0.0150	0.0430	0.3916

[1] Congeners coeluted in 2006 and 2007 but not in 2003; groups (years) cannot be compared.

[2] P-value for between year comparisons.

69

Table 10. Polybrominated diphenyl ether (PBDE), brominated biphenyl (BB)101, and hexabromocyclododecane (HBCD) concentrations (µg/kg wet weight) (including geometric means and comparisons) in osprey eggs from the lower Duwamish River (LDR), Washington, 2003 (N = 7), 2006–07 (N = 11).

[ND = not detected (less than detection limit), NA = not analyzed, NC = not calculated (>50% samples less than detection limit). Geometric means were calculated using one-half of the detection limit when >50% of the samples contained detectable residues]

Year-NestID	RM	ΣPBDE Congeners[2]	PBDE Congener[1]										154/ BB153	183	BB101	HBCD
			17	28	47	49	66	85	99	100	138	153				
2003-T18	0.0	211.05	NA	0.43	117.92	NA	NA	NA	36.77	27.76	0.16	12.07	15.62	0.33	ND	NA
2003-T105	0.4	199.73	NA	0.11	127.20	NA	NA	NA	25.66	20.70	0.13	10.37	15.38	0.17	ND	NA
2003-T115	1.2	439.22	NA	0.26	264.96	NA	NA	NA	55.30	38.36	0.21	34.42	45.24	0.46	ND	NA
2003-LCP	1.5	121.40	NA	0.11	72.34	NA	NA	NA	20.98	15.83	0.09	5.03	6.93	0.09	ND	NA
2003-HC	4.4	274.94	NA	0.52	162.31	NA	NA	NA	44.61	36.38	0.13	13.08	17.73	0.19	ND	NA
2003-112	5.7	155.11	NA	0.52	93.57	NA	NA	NA	30.93	17.99	0.09	5.06	6.80	0.15	ND	NA
2003-TCT	8.5	213.20	NA	0.20	136.45	NA	NA	NA	19.91	25.02	ND	13.03	18.39	0.20	ND	NA
2006-T18	0.0	732.20	4.65	71.18	201.43	166.24	2.22	ND	39.14	43.72	ND	21.73	25.86	ND	1.36	ND
2006-T104	0.1	187.83	2.54	4.15	115.62	ND	2.08	ND	21.31	25.69	ND	7.42	9.03	ND	ND	ND
2006-CSG	1.0	260.34	3.34	5.38	168.92	ND	1.45	ND	24.11	32.81	ND	10.75	13.59	ND	ND	ND
2006-T115	1.2	700.46	9.05	13.68	285.07	1.48	4.53	2.51	107.28	141.49	ND	68.78	66.54	ND	3.06	ND
2006-HC	4.4	411.86	5.83	8.43	210.67	ND	1.67	ND	73.13	55.99	ND	28.32	27.85	ND	ND	ND
2006-BDC	4.9	267.75	2.94	5.11	179.02	ND	1.72	ND	18.19	40.34	ND	9.68	10.59	ND	ND	ND
2006-CMP	5.7	619.43	15.29	23.83	315.44	3.06	4.15	1.96	90.39	90.37	ND	36.90	38.00	ND	1.61	ND
2007-T18	0.0	139.81	0.20	1.00	71.30	0.58	0.64	0.04	21.80	25.50	ND	8.32	10.05	0.12	0.38	ND
2007-T104	0.1	154.38	ND	0.46	84.40	0.36	0.56	0.03	23.50	25.60	ND	8.65	10.14	0.09	0.52	ND
2007-T105	0.4	186.43	0.09	0.82	99.00	0.69	0.92	0.06	32.10	31.30	ND	8.29	11.32	0.14	0.43	1.25
2007-CMP	5.7	538.87	0.12	1.11	247.60	0.95	1.53	0.12	95.80	93.40	0.33	46.75	47.15	0.62	1.72	1.59
2003		213.82	NA	0.26	129.04	NA	NA	NA	31.40	24.76	0.11	10.93	14.95	0.20	ND	NA
2006–07		298.51[3]	1.14	4.30	161.64	0.17	1.61	0.03	39.91	46.17	NC	16.97	19.17	NC	0.11	NC
P-value[4]		0.1992	-	0.0004	0.3371	-	-	-	0.4148	0.0238	-	0.2476	0.4694	-	-	-

[1]Congeners 190 and 209 were not detected in any samples.
[2]ΣPBDE = sum of congeners 17, 28, 47, 49, 66, 85, 99, 100, 138, 153, 154/BB153, 183, 190, and 209; eggs in 2003 were not analyzed for congeners 17, 49, 66, and 85, and HBCD.
[3]Sum of congeners 28, 47, 99, 100, 138, 153, 154/BB153 and 183 for comparison with 2003 eggs, which were not analyzed for four congeners (see footnote 2). Geometric mean of the sum of all congeners in 2006–07 eggs = 320.89 µg/kg wet weight.
[4]P-value for between year comparisons.

70

Table 11. Selected herbicide and fungicide (ng/kg wet weight) and mercury (mg/kg dry weight) concentrations (including geometric means and comparisons) in osprey eggs from the lower Duwamish River (LDR), 2003 (N = 7), 2006–07 (N = 11).

[ND = not detected (less than detection limit), NC = not calculated (>50% samples less than detection limit), T = trace (detected but not quantifiable), NA = not analyzed. Geometric means were calculated using one-half of the detection limit when >50% of the samples contained detectable residues]

| Year-NestID | RM | Herbicide/Fungicide[1] | | | Hg |
		Dimethyl-TCP[2]	Dacthal	Chlorothalonil	
2003-T18	0.0	14.06	ND	ND	1.70
2003-T105	0.4	9.24	ND	ND	0.26
2003-T115	1.2	16.15	ND	T	1.44
2003-LCP	1.5	11.50	5.09	ND	1.55
2003-HC	4.4	19.02	4.29	T	0.65
2003-112	5.7	10.01	ND	ND	0.43
2003-TCT	8.5	7.66	ND	T	0.37
2006-T18	0.0	173.63	1.61	171.84	NA[3]
2006-T104	0.1	120.42	ND	160.27	NA[3]
2006-CSG	1.0	90.17	ND	132.60	NA[3]
2006-T115	1.5	146.43	ND	440.96	NA[3]
2006-HC	4.4	58.95	1.65	249.16	NA[3]
2006-BDC	4.9	82.44	19.29	78.93	NA[3]
2006-CMP	5.7	79.89	ND	157.41	NA[3]
2007-T18	0.0	ND	ND	ND	0.42
2007-T104	0.1	ND	ND	ND	0.14
2007-T105	0.4	ND	ND	ND	0.46
2007-CMP	5.7	ND	ND	ND	ND
LDR 2003		11.97	NC	ND	0.72
LDR 2006–07		18.86[5]	NC	44.26	0.14[3]
P-value[4]		0.6212[5]	-	-	0.0453

[1] Other pesticides analyzed and not detected = atrazine, cyanazine, trichlopyr, simazine, alachlor, metolachlor, 24D, 24DB, 235T, MCPA, picloram, carbaryl and methomyl.

[2] An isomer of an unknown source.

[3] Hg analyzed in feathers not eggs in 2006, see table 16.

[4] P-value for between year comparisons.

[5] Geometric mean of Dimethyl-TCP using only 2006 data = 101.00 ng/kg wwt and was significantly different than 2003 means (11.97 ng/kg wwt) (P = <0.0001).

Table 12. Polybrominated diphenyl ether (PBDE), brominated biphenyl (BB)101, hexabromocyclododecane (HBCD) (μg/kg wet weight), and selected herbicide/fungicide concentrations (ng/kg wet weight) (including geometric means and comparisons) in osprey eggs from the lower Duwamish River, Washington (N = 11), and the Willamette River, Oregon (N = 10), 2006–07.

[D = lower Duwamish River, W = Willamette River, RM = river mile, ND = not detected (less than detection limit), NC = not calculated (>50% samples less than detection limit). Geometric means were calculated using one-half of the detection limit when >50% of the samples contained detectable residues]

River-NestID	RM	ΣPBDE Congeners[2]	PBDE Congeners[1]										
			17	28	47	49	66	85	99	100	138	153	183
D-T18	0.0	732.20	4.65	71.18	201.43	166.24	2.22	ND	39.14	43.72	ND	21.73	ND
D-T104	0.1	187.83	2.54	4.15	115.62	ND	2.08	ND	21.31	25.69	ND	7.42	ND
D-CSG	1.0	260.34	3.34	5.38	168.92	ND	1.45	ND	24.11	32.81	ND	10.75	ND
D-T115	1.5	700.46	9.05	13.68	285.07	1.48	4.53	2.51	107.28	141.49	ND	68.78	ND
D-HC	4.4	411.86	5.83	8.43	210.67	ND	1.67	ND	73.13	55.99	ND	28.32	ND
D-BDC	4.9	267.75	2.94	5.11	179.02	ND	1.72	ND	18.19	40.34	ND	9.68	ND
D-CMP	5.7	619.43	15.29	23.83	315.44	3.06	4.15	1.96	90.39	90.37	ND	36.90	ND
D-T18[3]	0.0	139.81	0.20	1.00	71.3	0.58	0.64	0.04	21.8	25.5	ND	8.32	0.12
D-T104[3]	0.1	154.38	ND	0.46	84.4	0.36	0.56	0.03	23.5	25.6	ND	8.65	0.09
D-T105[3]	0.4	186.43	0.09	0.82	99.0	0.69	0.92	0.06	32.1	31.3	ND	8.29	0.14
D-CMP[3]	5.7	538.87	0.12	1.11	247.6	0.95	1.53	0.12	95.8	93.4	0.33	46.75	0.62
W-15B	61.2	908.56	8.95	19.99	649.25	ND	ND	ND	25.89	147.48	ND	26.57	ND
W-21	66.2	1,612.78	17.05	38.49	1,017.13	ND	2.67	3.97	40.48	333.67	3.16	65.78	ND
W-30C	75.2	968.04	7.32	16.07	662.25	1.44	2.14	1.64	66.48	136.91	ND	33.01	ND
W-60	104.5	701.93	1.94	4.85	265.31	ND	ND	ND	11.21	396.17	ND	10.31	ND
W-79B	119.8	826.31	8.56	18.69	588.41	ND	ND	1.39	29.72	112.23	ND	33.37	ND
W-97D	135.3	507.46	4.29	9.40	372.54	ND	ND	ND	36.11	53.37	ND	16.19	ND
W-99A	137.9	697.65	6.34	14.72	499.39	ND	3.26	1.66	38.93	85.98	1.78	20.84	ND
W-111	145.9	599.12	4.83	8.46	390.81	1.81	3.43	ND	48.36	83.55	ND	33.62	ND
W-122	151.7	1,032.56	5.89	9.63	642.84	2.31	4.70	1.36	185.85	75.84	ND	65.23	ND
W-132A	157.3	1,880.78	13.81	25.82	988.33	3.80	9.64	1.86	498.08	196.84	ND	85.67	ND
Duwamish mean		320.89	1.14	4.30	161.64	0.17	1.61	0.03	39.91	46.17	NC	16.97	NC
Willamette mean		897.44	6.76	14.17	562.19	NC	0.20	0.13	52.05	132.87	NC	32.36	ND
P-value[4]		0.0003	0.0241	0.0358	<0.0001	-	0.0905	0.2414	0.5014	0.0010	-	0.0622	-

[1]Congeners 190 and 209 were not detected in any samples.
[2]ΣPBDE = sum of congeners 17, 28, 47, 49, 66, 85, 99, 100, 138, 153, 154/BB153, 183, 190, and 209.
[3]Eggs sampled and analyzed in 2007, all other nests sampled in 2006.
[4]Comparison between Duwamish and Willamette means.

72

Table 12. Polybrominated diphenyl ether (PBDE), brominated biphenyl (BB)101, hexabromocyclododecane (HBCD) (µg/kg wet weight), and selected herbicide/fungicide concentrations (ng/kg wet weight) (including geometric means and comparisons) in osprey eggs from the lower Duwamish River, Washington (N = 11), and the Willamette River, Oregon (N = 10), 2006–07.—Continued

[Geometric means were calculated using one-half of the detection limit when >50% of the samples contained detectable residues. D = lower Duwamish River, W = Willamette River, RM = river mile, ND = not detected (less than detection limit), NC = not calculated (>50% samples less than detection limit)]

River-NestID	RM	PBDE/BB Congeners		HBCD	Selected herbicides/fungicide[1]		
		BB101	154/BB153		Dacthal	Dimethyl-TCP[2]	Chlorothalonil
D-T18	0.0	1.36	25.86	ND	1.61	173.63	171.84
D-T104	0.1	ND	9.03	ND	ND	120.42	160.27
D-CSG	1.0	ND	13.59	ND	ND	90.17	132.60
D-T115	1.5	3.06	66.54	ND	ND	146.43	440.96
D-HC	4.4	ND	27.85	ND	1.65	58.95	249.16
D-BDC	4.9	ND	10.59	ND	19.29	82.44	78.93
D-CMP	5.7	1.61	38.00	ND	ND	79.89	157.41
D-T18[3]	0.0	0.38	10.05	ND	ND	ND	ND
D-T104[3]	0.1	0.52	10.14	ND	ND	ND	ND
D-T105[3]	0.4	0.43	11.32	1.25	ND	ND	ND
D-CMP[3]	5.7	1.72	47.15	1.59	ND	ND	ND
W-15B	61.2	ND	30.40	ND	12.54	40.37	8.59
W-21	66.2	ND	90.34	ND	ND	34.32	73.92
W-30C	75.2	0.22	40.81	ND	ND	37.90	9.06
W-60	104.5	ND	12.15	ND	ND	145.86	45.47
W-79B	119.8	ND	33.96	ND	ND	90.4	21.41
W-97D	135.3	ND	15.56	ND	25.65	121.10	12.62
W-99A	137.9	ND	24.77	ND	ND	19.05	17.32
W-111	145.9	ND	24.25	ND	23.18	104.53	68.28
W-122	151.7	ND	41.38	ND	5.07	3,478.14	40.90
W-132A	157.3	ND	56.89	ND	3.74	2,436.88	21.58
Duwamish mean		0.11	19.17	NC	NC	18.86	44.26
Willamette mean		NC	31.68	ND	1.27	130.34	24.37
P-value[4]		-	0.0989	-	-	0.0477	0.3786

[1] Other pesticides (atrazine, cyanazine, trichlopyr, simazine, alachlor, metolachlor, 24D, 24DB, 235T, MCPA, picloram, carbaryl and methomyl) were analyzed in 2003 and not detected and thus were not analyzed in eggs in 2006–07.

[2] An isomer of unknown source.

[3] Eggs sampled and analyzed in 2007, all other nests sampled in 2006.

[4] Comparison between Duwamish and Willamette means.

73

Table 13. Morphological measurements of osprey nestlings from the lower Duwamish River, Washington and the Willamette River, Oregon, 2006–07.

River-NestID[1]	Nestling Number	Date	Age (days)[2]	Crop Size[3]	Mass (g)	Wing Chord (mm)	8th Primary (mm)	Rectix (mm)	Band #	Blood	Feather
D-T18	1	08/13/07	46	4	1,439	359	231	155	608-74574	YES	YES
D-T18	2	08/13/07	[4]	4	1,391	346	211	138	608-74577	NO	NO
D-T104	1	07/11/07	35	3	1,341	300	168	97	608-74574	YES	YES
D-CSG	1	08/03/06	[4]	4	1,482	311	198	121	608-74571	YES	YES
D-CSG	2	08/03/06	43	4	1,540	324	209	130	608-74572	NO	NO
D-T115	1	07/27/06	40	2	1,740	296	181	114	608-74567	YES	YES
D-T115	2	07/27/06	[4]	3	1,469	314	199	119	608-74568	NO	NO
D-HC	1	07/27/06	[4]	4	1,497	390	269	170	608-74566	YES	YES
D-BDC	1	08/02/06	46	4	1,529	350	229	148	608-74570	YES	YES
D-BDC	2	08/02/06	[4]	3	1,509	335	223	139	608-74569	NO	NO
D-CMP	1	07/11/07	35	4	1,660	342	210	148	608-74573	YES	YES
D-CMP	2	07/11/07	[4]	4	1,331	328	201	134	608-74574	NO	NO
W-15B	1	07/19/06	[4]	4	1,462	335	221	136	--	NO	NO
W-15B	2	07/19/06	41	3	1,804	332	194	116	608-74563	YES	YES
W-21	1	07/19/06	43	3	1,772	349	210	131	608-74562	YES	YES
W-30C	1	07/19/06	43	4	1,475	338	211	125	608-74561	YES	YES
W-79B	1	07/06/06	[4]	4	1,673	362	250	177	--	NO	NO
W-79B	2	07/06/06	[4]	4	1,337	356	236	153	608-74559	YES	YES
W-111	1	07/20/06	[4]	4	1,336	356	230	153	608-74565	NO	NO
W-111	2	07/20/06	50	4	1,684	390	254	154	608-74564	YES	YES
W-122	1	07/07/06	45	4	1,721	331	223	137	608-74560	YES	NO
Duwamish mean[5]			40.8	3.6	1,527	335	212	136			
Willamette mean[5]			44.4	3.7	1,632	349	221	136			
P-value[6]			0.21	0.81	0.26	0.42	0.59	0.99			

[1] D = Lower Duwamish River, W = Willamette.

[2] Estimated age (± 3 days) determined by back-calculation from sampling date to hatching date.

[3] 1-Full, 4=empty.

[4] Is not determined.

[5] Arithmetic means.

[6] P-value for comparison between Duwamish and Willamette means.

Table 14. Mean hematological and biochemical determinations in osprey nestlings sampled from the lower Duwamish River (LDR), Washington and Willamette River (WR), Oregon, 2006–07.

Parameter[1]	Group[2]	Unit	LDR (N = 7) mean	LDR (N = 7) range	WR (N = 6) mean	WR (N = 6) range	P-value[3]
Age	Mor		40.8	(35-46)	44.4	(38-50)	0.2133
Hematocrit	RBC	%	34.0	(28-39)	28.5	(27-30)	0.0110
WBC	WBC	x10³/μL	11.3	(6-16)	10.7	(7-23)	0.8315
Lymphocytes	WBC	%	26.6	(12-40)	17.7	(6-27)	0.1067
Heterophils	WBC	%	63.7	(52-81)	79.2	(70-87)	0.0090
Eosinophils	WBC	%	9.9	(5-15)	2.7	(1-7)	0.0029
Monocytes	WBC	%	0.1	(0-1)	0.5	(0-2)	-
Albumin	PP	g/dL	1.3	(0.9-1.6)	1.4	(1.2-1.6)	0.3313
Pre-albumin	PP	g/dL	0.09	(0.07-0.11)	0.18	(0.09-0.54)	0.0363
α-1 globulins	PP	g/dL	0.14	(0.08-0.38)	0.10	(0.07-0.14)	0.1523
α-2 globulins	PP	g/dL	0.22	(0.11-0.48)	0.17	(0.14-0.20)	0.3345
β globulins	PP	g/dL	0.67	(0.38-0.92)	1.19	(0.95-1.35)	0.0004
γ globulins	PP	g/dL	0.24	(0.15-0.44)	0.41	(0.25-0.55)	0.0148
AGR	PP		1.18	(0.82-1.45)	0.88	(0.68-1.0)	0.0290
Total plasma protein	PP/Met	g/dL	2.8	(2.4-3.0)	3.5	(2.8-4.0)	0.0091
Amylase	Met	IU/L	305.7	(279-343)	335.7	(314-391)	0.1900
Bile acids	Met	μmol/L	21.0[4]	(11.2-38.2)	15.8	(3.1-36.5)	0.5200
BUN	Met	mg/dL	5.6	(2.0-8.3)	6.4	(2.0-12.1)	0.6035
Creatinine	Met	mg/dL	0.40	(0.26-0.58)	0.38	(0.25-0.56)	0.6933
BCR	Met		16.3[4]	(6.4-32.5)	11.6	(5.7-20)	0.3186
Calcium	Met	mg/dL	9.8	(9.2-10.6)	10.0	(8.7-10.9)	0.7362
Cholesterol	Met	mg/dL	145	(124-201)	128	(100-153)	0.2208
Glucose	Met	mg/dL	330	(293-389)	279	(255-304)	0.0047
Lipase	Met	IU/L	122.1	(57-230)	142.0	(96-207)	0.5710
Phosphorus	Met	mg/dL	7.9	(6.4-10.8)	7.1	(6.3-8.0)	0.2760
Triglycerides	Met	mg/dL	71	(28-150)	140	(57-523)	0.1336
Uric acid	Met	mg/dL	13.9	(11.2-15.2)	9.7	(5.9-16.5)	0.0491
CO₂	E	mmol/L	28.4[4]	(27-32)	25.8	(22-29)	0.1118
Potassium	E	mmol/L	2.3[4]	(1.9-3.0)	3.2	(2.3-3.9)	0.0290
Sodium	E	mmol/L	139.2[4]	(137-142)	139.5	(137-144)	0.8387
T4	H	μg/dL	1.1	(0.7-1.7)	1.4	(0.6-1.7)	0.2684
Alk Phos	TE	IU/L	259	(88-360)	260	(194-384)	0.9884
ALT	TE	IU/L	30	(15-41)	45	(11-68)	0.1559
AST	TE	IU/L	33	(20-45)	20	(13-35)	0.0251
BCHE	TE	IU/L	794	(432-1,510)	568	(463-764)	0.1739
CK	TE	IU/L	2,493	(1,953-3,498)	1,964	(1,683-2,355)	0.0546
GGT	TE	IU/L	9.0	(0-15)	8.6	(0-11)	0.8576
GSSGred	TE	IU/L	155	(103-278)	155	(113-298)	0.9946
LDH	TE	IU/L	2,664	(1,761-4,468)	2,677	(1,632-4,767)	0.9850
LDH-L	TE	IU/L	432	(317-673)	470	(370-650)	0.5506
S-GSHpx	TE	IU/L	10,636	(7,950-13,411)	6,095	(4,632-7,051)	0.0005
T-GSHpx	TE	IU/L	15,885	(15,260-16,799)	11,127	(8,036-13,100)	0.0001

[1]Log and unlogged values used to calculate means. WBC=white blood cells, AGR=albumin/globulin ratio, BUN=blood urea nitrogen, BCR=blood urea nitrogen/creatinine ratio, CO₂=carbon dioxide, T4=hormone thyroxine, Alk Phos=alkaline phosphatase, ALT=alanine aminotransferase, AST=aspartate aminotransferase, BCHE=butyrylcholinesterase, CK=creatine kinase, GGT=gamma-glutamyl transpeptidase, GSSGred=glutathione reductase, LDH=lactate dehydrogenase, LDH-L=lactate dehydrogenase-L, S-GSHpx=selenium-dependent glutathione peroxidase, T-GSHpx=total glutathione peroxidase.

[2]Mor = morphometric, RBC = red blood cells, WBC = white blood cells, PP = plasma proteins (immune system), MET = metabolites, E = electrolytes, H = hormone, TE = tissue enzymes.

[3]P-value for comparison of Duwamish and Willamette means.

[4]BCR N = 6, sodium N = 5, potassium N = 5, CO₂ N = 5, bile acids N = 5.

Table 15. Polychlorinated biphenyl (PCB) concentrations (μg/kg wet weight) (including geometric means and comparisons) in osprey nestling plasma from the lower Duwamish River, Washington (N = 7), and the Willamette River, Oregon (N = 6), 2006–07.

[D = lower Duwamish River, W = Willamette River, RM = river mile, ND = not detected (less than detection limit), NC = not calculated (>50% samples less than detection limit). Geometric means were calculated using one-half of the detection limit when >50% of the samples contained detectable residues]

| River-NestID | RM | Total PCBs | | PCB Congener[1] | | | | | | | | | | | |
		ΣPCB Congeners	Aroclor 1254:1260	31/28	44	49	52	64	56/60	66/95	70/76	74	87	97	99
D-CSG	1.0	37.26	73.29	ND	ND	ND	0.40	ND	0.43	0.52	ND	ND	0.56	0.66	1.05
D-T115	1.5	36.32	74.91	ND	ND	ND	0.62	ND	0.33	0.38	ND	1.40	0.68	0.40	1.37
D-HC	4.4	31.71	73.67	ND	ND	ND	ND	ND	ND	ND	ND	ND	ND	0.54	0.92
D-BDC	4.9	26.86	55.99	ND	ND	0.14	0.59	ND	ND	0.47	ND	ND	0.56	0.45	0.90
D-T18[2]	0.0	32.43	69.37	3.64	ND	0.47	0.90	ND	0.26	0.89	0.33	0.79	ND	0.35	0.89
D-T104[2]	0.1	51.90	137.92	3.25	0.26	0.39	0.87	0.19	0.36	1.29	0.29	0.55	ND	0.73	0.31
D-CMP[2]	5.7	84.07	241.36	2.73	1.10	1.14	2.07	1.35	0.69	1.87	0.50	1.06	ND	1.28	2.07
W-15B	61.2	12.29	27.35	ND	ND	ND	ND	ND	ND	0.35	ND	ND	ND	ND	0.46
W-21	66.2	8.52	16.35	ND	ND	0.41	ND	ND	ND	0.54	ND	ND	ND	ND	0.37
W-30C	75.2	4.26	12.50	ND	ND	0.18	ND	ND	ND	ND	ND	ND	ND	ND	ND
W79B	119.8	8.95	18.47	ND	ND	0.12	0.42	ND	ND	0.38	ND	ND	ND	0.44	0.48
W-111	145.9	2.82	12.45	ND	ND	ND	ND	ND	ND	ND	ND	ND	ND	ND	ND
W-122	151.7	9.21	24.00	ND	ND	ND	ND	ND	ND	ND	ND	ND	ND	ND	0.35
Duwamish mean		39.98	91.15	NC	NC	0.17	0.53	NC	0.22	0.52	NC	0.90	NC	0.58	0.94
Willamette mean		6.85	17.71	ND	ND	0.10	NC	ND	ND	0.14	ND	ND	ND	NC	0.20
P-value[3]		<0.0001	<0.0001	-	-	0.4395	-	-	-	0.0766	-	-	-	-	0.0081

[1]PCB congener 42 was detected in only one Duwamish sample (CMP: 0.56 μg/kg).
[2]Nests sampled in 2007, all other nests sampled in 2006.
[3]P-value for comparison of Duwamish and Willamette means.

Table 15. Polychlorinated biphenyl (PCB) concentrations (µg/kg wet weight) (including geometric means and comparisons) in osprey nestling plasma from the lower Duwamish River, Washington (N = 7), and the Willamette River, Oregon (N = 6), 2006–07.—Continued

[D = lower Duwamish River, W = Willamette River, RM = river mile, ND = not detected (less than detection limit), NC = not calculated (>50% samples less than detection limit). Geometric means were calculated using one-half of the detection limit when >50% of the samples contained detectable residues]

River-NestID	RM	PCB Congener												
		101	105	110	118	128	138	141	146	149	151	153	158	172
D-CSG	1.0	1.75	ND	1.44	2.41	0.80	5.42	ND	0.70	1.90	0.30	5.28	ND	0.16
D-T115	1.5	1.75	ND	1.26	2.20	0.70	5.54	ND	0.71	1.66	ND	5.18	ND	0.17
D-HC	4.4	1.67	ND	1.45	2.13	0.68	5.45	ND	0.71	1.81	ND	5.15	ND	ND
D-BDC	4.9	1.57	ND	1.18	1.71	0.54	4.14	ND	0.51	1.62	0.26	3.79	ND	ND
D-T18[1]	0.0	1.23	0.20	0.85	0.98	0.47	3.38	0.33	0.42	1.19	0.25	2.91	ND	0.41
D-T104[1]	0.1	2.40	0.37	1.31	2.04	1.12	6.71	0.75	0.88	2.71	0.53	5.85	0.50	0.32
D-CMP[1]	5.7	3.96	0.61	2.07	3.57	0.96	11.75	1.65	1.54	4.65	0.70	9.83	0.87	0.67
W-15B	61.2	0.78	ND	0.73	1.29	0.08	2.02	ND	0.27	0.72	ND	2.10	ND	ND
W-21	66.2	0.80	ND	0.46	1.03	ND	1.21	ND	0.13	0.56	ND	1.18	ND	ND
W-30C	75.2	0.53	ND	0.32	ND	ND	0.93	ND	ND	ND	ND	0.76	ND	ND
W79B	119.8	0.86	ND	0.68	1.10	0.21	1.37	ND	ND	0.61	ND	1.13	ND	ND
W-111	145.9	0.33	ND	0.28	ND	ND	0.92	ND	ND	ND	ND	0.58	ND	ND
W-122	151.7	0.66	ND	0.43	1.31	0.36	1.78	ND	ND	0.52	ND	1.53	ND	ND
Duwamish mean		1.91	NC	1.32	2.02	0.72	5.64	NC	0.72	2.02	0.21	5.10	NC	0.18
Willamette mean		0.63	ND	0.46	0.41	0.10	1.31	ND	NC	0.26	ND	1.11	ND	ND
P-value[2]		0.0002	-	0.0001	0.0286	0.0001	<0.0001	-	-	0.0022	-	<0.0001	-	-

[1]Nests sampled in 2007, all other nests sampled in 2006.

[2]P-value for comparison of Duwamish and Willamette means.

Table 15. Polychlorinated biphenyl (PCB) concentrations (µg/kg wet weight) (including geometric means and comparisons) in osprey nestling plasma from the lower Duwamish River, Washington (N = 7), and the Willamette River, Oregon (N = 6), 2006–07.—Continued

[D = lower Duwamish River, W = Willamette River, RM = river mile, ND = not detected (less than detection limit), NC = not calculated (>50% samples less than detection limit). Geometric means were calculated using one-half of the detection limit when >50% of the samples contained detectable residues]

River-NestID	RM	PCB Congener												
		174	170/190	171/156	177	180	183	187	194	195	200	201	203	206
D-CSG	1.0	0.73	0.80	0.50	0.60	3.46	0.91	2.66	0.74	0.32	ND	1.24	0.82	0.43
D-T115	1.5	0.53	0.64	0.42	0.58	3.27	0.88	2.71	0.48	ND	ND	0.96	0.60	0.90
D-HC	4.4	0.62	0.55	0.43	0.62	3.64	0.87	2.45	0.52	ND	ND	0.89	0.63	ND
D-BDC	4.9	0.54	0.48	0.35	0.45	2.12	0.58	1.90	0.44	ND	ND	0.77	0.51	0.27
D-T18[1]	0.0	1.35	1.08	0.73	0.57	1.74	1.06	2.38	0.25	ND	ND	0.37	0.96	0.05
D-T104[1]	0.1	0.90	1.87	1.13	0.91	3.29	1.55	2.43	0.95	0.47	0.36	1.19	0.96	0.34
D-CMP[1]	5.7	1.72	2.23	1.52	1.25	5.75	2.07	3.95	1.16	0.49	0.35	1.69	1.55	0.13
W-15B	61.2	ND	0.23	ND	ND	1.22	0.29	1.13	ND	ND	ND	0.40	0.22	ND
W-21	66.2	ND	0.14	ND	ND	0.53	ND	0.79	ND	ND	ND	ND	ND	ND
W-30C	75.2	ND	ND	ND	ND	0.38	ND	0.71	ND	ND	ND	ND	ND	ND
W79B	119.8	ND	ND	ND	ND	0.44	ND	0.73	ND	ND	ND	ND	ND	ND
W-111	145.9	ND	ND	ND	ND	0.41	ND	ND	ND	ND	ND	ND	ND	ND
W-122	151.7	ND	0.14	0.50	ND	0.74	ND	0.91	ND	ND	ND	ND	ND	ND
Duwamish mean		0.83	0.93	0.63	0.67	3.12	1.05	2.58	0.58	NC	NC	0.93	0.81	0.20
Willamette mean		ND	0.09	NC	ND	0.57	NC	0.52	ND	ND	ND	NC	NC	ND
P-value[2]		-	<0.0001	-	-	<0.0001	-	0.0044	-	-	-	-	-	-

[1]Nests sampled in 2007, all other nests sampled in 2006.
[2]P-value for comparison of Duwamish and Willamette means.

Table 16. Organochlorine contaminant concentrations (µg/kg wet weight) (including geometric means and comparisons) in osprey nestling plasma from the lower Duwamish River, Washington (N = 7), and the Willamette River, Oregon (N = 6), 2006–07.

[D = lower Duwamish River, W = Willamette River, RM = river mile, QCB = pentachlorobenzene, HCB = hexachlorobenzene, TransNon = *trans*-nonachlor, OxyChlor = oxychlordane, CisChlor = *cis*-chlordane, CisNon = *cis*-nonachlor, TotChlor = total chlordanes: sum of *trans*-nonachlor, *cis*-nonachlor, oxychlordane, *trans*-chlordane, *cis*-chlordane, DDT = *p,p'*-DDT, DDE = *p,p'*-DDE, DDD = *p,p'*-DDD, HE = heptachlor epoxide, ND = not detected (less than detection limit), NC = not calculated (>50% samples less than detection limit). TCB1245 (1,2,4,5-tetrachlorobenzene), OCS (octachlorostyrene), α-, β-, γ-hexachlorocyclohexane (HCH), and *trans*-Chlordane were not detected in any samples. TCB1234 (1,2,3,4-tetrachlorobenzene) was detected in one sample: W-30C (0.355 µg/kg). Geometric means were calculated using one-half of the detection limit when >50% of the samples contained detectable residues]

River-NestID	Year	RM	QCB	HCB	Mirex	TransNon	OxyChlor	CisChlor	CisNon	TotChlor	DDT	DDE	DDD	HE	Dieldrin
D-CSG	2006	1.0	ND	ND	ND	2.27	0.39	0.26	1.50	4.41	ND	7.35	1.38	ND	0.97
D-T115	2006	1.5	ND	ND	ND	0.96	0.27	ND	0.65	1.87	ND	4.61	0.55	ND	0.57
D-HC	2006	4.4	ND	1.23	ND	0.73	0.41	ND	1.21	2.34	ND	8.02	1.08	1.64	0.61
D-BDC	2006	4.9	ND	0.34	ND	1.82	0.30	ND	0.92	3.04	1.39	5.77	1.01	ND	0.82
D-T18	2007	0.0	0.35	0.62	ND	0.96	0.16	0.59	0.56	2.27	ND	5.19	1.54	ND	ND
D-T104	2007	0.1	0.42	1.08	0.55	2.56	0.28	1.13	1.51	5.47	0.20	9.41	1.83	0.31	1.75
D-CMP	2007	5.7	0.95	3.18	ND	4.99	0.72	2.31	3.60	11.62	0.98	20.66	5.63	0.66	3.29
W-15B	2006	61.2	ND	0.49	ND	1.11	0.39	ND	0.52	2.02	3.42	53.65	4.39	ND	5.81
W-21	2006	66.2	ND	0.76	ND	1.03	0.50	0.30	0.46	2.29	4.99	20.59	4.18	2.31	7.79
W-30C	2006	75.2	ND	0.22	ND	4.49	0.75	1.14	1.97	8.34	3.91	12.44	2.30	1.70	3.49
W79B	2006	119.8	ND	0.53	ND	0.71	0.20	ND	0.28	1.19	ND	4.49	ND	ND	1.03
W-111	2006	145.9	ND	0.14	ND	0.27	ND	ND	0.20	0.47	ND	3.43	ND	ND	0.73
W-122	2006	151.7	ND	0.31	ND	0.79	ND	ND	ND	0.79	ND	6.74	0.44	ND	1.03
Duwamish mean			NC	0.42	NC	1.67	0.33	0.24	1.19	3.64	NC	7.68	1.44	NC	0.61
Willamette mean			ND	0.35	ND	0.96	0.21	NC	0.33	1.60	0.45	10.61	0.60	NC	2.23
P-value[1]			-	0.8097	-	0.2364	0.3567	-	0.0325	0.1009	-	0.4770	0.3181	-	0.1208

[1]P-value for comparison of Duwamish and Willamette means.

79

Table 17. Polybrominated diphenyl ether (PBDE), brominated biphenyl (BB) 101, and selected herbicide and fungicide contaminant concentrations (µg/kg wet weight) in osprey nestling plasma, and mercury (Hg) (µg/kg dry weight) in feathers (including geometric means and comparisons), from the lower Duwamish River, Washington (N = 7) and the Willamette River, Oregon (N = 6), 2006–07.

[D = lower Duwamish River, W = Willamette River, RM = river mile, ND = not detected (less than detection limit), NC = not calculated (>50% samples less than detection limit). Geometric means were calculated using one-half of the detection limit when >50% of the samples contained detectable residues]

| River-NestID | Year | RM | ΣPBDE[2] | PBDE Congeners[1] | | | | | | | | | BB101 | Chlor[3] | Di-TCP[4] | Dacthal | Hg |
				28	47	49	99	100	153	154/BB153	183					
D-CSG	2006	1.0	6.91	ND	4.75	ND	0.83	0.81	0.26	0.26	ND	ND	ND	ND	ND	2,220
D-T115	2006	1.5	5.29	ND	3.55	ND	0.79	0.54	0.20	0.21	ND	ND	ND	0.01	ND	1,490
D-HC	2006	4.4	5.50	ND	3.86	ND	0.55	0.59	0.20	0.22	0.09	ND	ND	0.03	ND	2,660
D-BDC	2006	4.9	5.08	ND	3.56	ND	0.55	0.58	0.20	0.18	ND	ND	ND	ND	ND	2,630
D-T18	2007	0.0	2.39	ND	1.19	0.05	0.56	0.30	0.11	0.13	ND	ND	ND	ND	ND	NA
D-T104	2007	0.1	9.72	0.20	6.01	0.16	0.40	1.79	0.44	0.62	ND	ND	ND	ND	ND	NA
D-CMP	2007	5.7	15.56	0.28	9.05	0.23	1.60	2.59	0.76	0.92	ND	ND	ND	ND	ND	NA
W-15B	2006	61.2	39.61	0.28	32.33	ND	1.42	3.86	0.71	1.00	ND	ND	ND	0.004	ND	745
W-21	2006	66.2	28.46	0.36	24.02	0.06	0.26	2.67	0.48	0.61	ND	ND	ND	ND	ND	4,300
W-30C	2006	75.2	8.76	ND	7.34	ND	0.33	0.78	0.16	0.16	ND	ND	ND	0.02	ND	3,420
W79B	2006	119.8	27.28	ND	22.96	ND	0.95	2.24	0.50	0.62	ND	ND	ND	ND	ND	2,810
W-111	2006	145.9	11.99	ND	10.37	ND	0.27	0.98	0.13	0.25	ND	ND	ND	ND	ND	2,210
W-122	2006	151.7	36.47	0.20	28.48	0.49	0.94	3.48	1.79	1.09	ND	0.083	ND	0.02	ND	NA
Duwamish mean			6.24	NC	3.95	NC	0.68	0.80	0.26	0.29	NC	ND	ND	NC[4]	ND	2,193
Willamette mean			22.14	0.05	18.39	NC	0.56	1.99	0.43	0.51	ND	NC	ND	NC[4]	ND	2,325
P-value[5]			0.0030	-	0.0009	-	0.5458	0.0424	0.2808	0.1910	-	-	-	-	-	0.8772

[1]HBCD (hexabromocyclododecane) and PBDE congeners 17, 85, 138, 190, 209 were not detected in any samples; congener 66 only detected in two LDR samples (2007: CMP and T104 both 0.08 µg/kg ww).

[2]ΣPBDE = sum of congeners 17, 28, 47, 49, 66, 85, 99, 100, 138, 153, 154/BB153, 183, 190, and 209.

[3]Chlorothalonil.

[4]Di-TCP (dimethyl-TCP) was not detected in any plasma samples, obtained values area a result of sample workup, thus means were not calculated.

[5]P-value for comparison of Duwamish and Willamette means.

Table 18. Significant Pearson correlation coefficients ($\alpha = 0.05$) for contaminant residues and biochemical/hematological chemistries (logged/unlogged values used) in osprey nestling (~35–45 days old) blood plasma from the lower Duwamish River (N = 7), Washington, and the Willamette River (N = 6), Oregon, 2006–07.

| Contaminant[12] | Morphometrics[23] | | | RBC[2] | WBC differentials | | | Immune[23] | | | | Plasma proteins | | | Hormone |
	% Lipid[4]	Mass	8th Primary	Hemat	Eosin	Hetero	Lymph	AGR	α1G	α2G	βG	γG	PreAlb[5]	TPP	T4
HCB							0.63								-0.62
p,p'-DDE															
p,p'-DDD															
Dieldrin				-0.60		0.60									
trans-nonachlor									0.62						
cis-nonachlor	-0.67								0.59			-0.55		-0.62	
Total Chlordanes	—														
PCB66/95			-0.56							0.62					
PCB97	-0.61	-0.55		0.60		-0.68					-0.87	-0.69		-0.81	
PCB99				0.56		-0.57						-0.62			
PCB101				0.57		-0.57			0.58		-0.76	-0.78		-0.66	
PCB110					0.55	-0.57					-0.74	-0.84	-0.63	-0.74	
PCB118								0.54				-0.65			
PCB128				0.58	0.55	-0.60			0.54		-0.80	-0.60		-0.64	
PCB138					0.55	-0.56					-0.80	-0.73		-0.65	
PCB146					0.60						-0.68	-0.80	-0.56	-0.63	
PCB149						-0.58					-0.65	-0.72		-0.56	
PCB153					0.56						-0.74	-0.78		-0.64	
PCB156/171				0.57		-0.61			0.64		-0.81				
PCB174				0.66	0.67	-0.70			0.55		-0.88	-0.60		-0.67	
PCB177				0.63	0.69	-0.67		0.57			-0.87	-0.66		-0.70	
PCB170/190						-0.55			0.60		-0.74	-0.63			
PCB180				0.56	0.60	-0.51					-0.75	-0.75	-0.55	-0.64	
PCB183				0.56	0.61	-0.55					-0.77	-0.73		-0.71	
PCB187												-0.69			
PCB194				0.58	0.66	-0.60		0.62			-0.85	-0.71		-0.70	
PCB201					0.62						-0.69	-0.80		-0.70	
PCB203				0.59	0.61	-0.57					-0.77	-0.71		-0.70	
Aroclor 1260				0.55	0.59	-0.59			0.63		-0.75	-0.75	-0.55	-0.64	
Aroclor 5460									0.58		-0.84	-0.67		-0.65	
ΣPCB						-0.61					-0.79	-0.73		-0.65	
BDE47	0.66			-0.64	-0.78	0.64					0.64		0.55		
BDE100	0.62			-0.57	-0.77										
BDE153	0.62				-0.57										
BDE154/153	0.59				-0.69										
ΣPBDE	0.68			-0.62	-0.81	0.59					0.57				
Hg (N = 9)															

81

[1] Represents contaminants with quantifiable concentrations in > 50% of samples, and one-half of the detection limit was used for samples containing non-detect residues for statistical analyses. N=13 unless indicated otherwise.

[2] HCB = hexachlorobenzene, total chlordanes = sum of *trans*-nonachlor, *cis*-nonachlor, oxychlordane, *trans*-chlordane, *cis*-chlordane, PCB = polychlorinated biphenyls, Aroclor 5460 = Aroclor 1254:1260, BDE = brominated diphenyl ether, PBDE = polybrominated diphenyl ethers, Hg = total mercury, RBC = red blood cells, Hemat = hematocrit (% packed cell volume), Eosin = eosinophils, Hetero = heterophils, Lymph = lymphocytes, AGR = albumin/globulin ratio, α1G = alpha1 globulins, α2G = alpha2 globulins, βG = beta globulins, γG = gamma globulins, PreAlb = prealbumin, TPP = total plasma protein, T4 = thyroxine.

[3] No significant associations were observed between any contaminant and wing chord (morphometric; used as surrogate for nestling age in addition to 8th Primary), albumin and white blood cells (immune).

[4] in plasma.

[5] Spearman correlations.

82

Table 18. Significant Pearson correlation coefficients (α = 0.05) for contaminant residues and biochemical/hematological chemistries (logged/unlogged values used) in osprey nestling (~35-45 days old) blood plasma from the lower Duwamish River (N = 7), Washington, and the Willamette River (N = 6), Oregon, 2006–07.—Continued

Contaminant[12]	Tissue Enzymes[23]							Metabolites[23]						Electrolytes[23]	
	TGSHpx	SGSHpx	AST	BCHE	AMYL	BILE[4]	BCR	Ca	CHOL	CREA	GLUC	TRIG	URIC	K[4]	CO2[4]
HCB				0.57											
p,p'-DDE					0.62										
p,p'-DDD	0.72					0.64									
Dieldrin			-0.63				-0.67			-0.59					
trans-nonachlor	0.58														
cis-nonachlor	0.66	0.55											0.63		0.67
Total Chlordanes	0.68												0.57		
PCB66/95															
PCB97	0.60	0.64	0.68		-0.59						0.73				
PCB99	0.59	0.61									0.72	-0.64			
PCB101	0.81	0.72									0.70				
PCB110	0.77	0.76									0.78				
PCB118											0.58				
PCB128	0.66	0.67	0.59								0.74				
PCB138	0.84	0.77									0.77				
PCB146	0.90	0.78									0.66		0.62	-0.68	
PCB149	0.66	0.62									0.63				
PCB153	0.86	0.79									0.76				
PCB156/171	0.77	0.65									0.61				
PCB174	0.87	0.76	0.62	0.57							0.70			-0.66	
PCB177	0.88	0.79	0.59								0.73			-0.67	
PCB170/190	0.89	0.71									0.69				
PCB180	0.88	0.80									0.77				
PCB183	0.90	0.76									0.71	-0.55	0.68	-0.60	
PCB187	0.78	0.66									0.56		0.56	-0.65	
PCB194	0.86	0.83									0.72	-0.57		-0.65	
PCB201	0.88	0.82									0.73	-0.58	0.70	-0.62	
PCB203	0.90	0.77									0.71		0.67	-0.64	
Aroclor1260	0.88	0.80									0.77			-0.60	
Aroclor5460	0.84	0.69		0.63					0.57		0.71			-0.61	
ΣPCB	0.85	0.73									0.72				
BDE47	-0.67	-0.58	-0.68												-0.65
BDE99											0.55				-0.66
BDE100					0.64										-0.67
BDE153					0.62										-0.69
BDE154/153					0.62										-0.67
ΣPBDE	-0.62	-0.57	-0.64		0.58										
Hg (N = 9)								0.77							

83

[1]All contaminants logged; represents contaminants with quantifiable concentrations in > 50% of samples, and one-half of the detection limit was used for samples containing non-detect residues for statistical analyses. No significant correlations were observed between biochemistries and oxychlordane. N=13 unless indicated otherwise.

[2]HCB = hexachlorobenzene, total chlordanes = sum of *trans*-nonachlor, *cis*-nonachlor, oxychlordane, *trans*-chlordane, *cis*-chlordane, PCB = polychlorinated biphenyls, Aroclor 5460 = Aroclor 1254:1260, BDE = brominated diphenyl ether, PBDE = polybrominated diphenyl ethers, Hg = total mercury, TGSHpx = total glutathione peroxidase, SGSHpx = selenium dependent glutathione peroxidase, AST = aspartate aminotransferase, BCHE = butyrylcholinesterase, AMYL = amylase, BILE = bile acids, BCR = blood urea nitrogen/creatinine ratio, BUN = blood urea nitrogen, Ca = calcium, CHOL = cholesterol, CREA = creatinine, GLUC = glucose, TRIG = triglycerides, URIC = uric acid, K = potassium, CO_2 = carbon dioxide (bicarbonate).

[3]No significant associations were observed between any contaminant and enzymes: alkaline phosphatase, lactate dehydrogenase-L, gamma-glutamyl transpeptidase, alanine aminotransferase, glutathione reductase; metabolites: blood urea nitrogen, lipase, phosphorus; and electrolyte: sodium.

[4]N: BILE = 10, K = 11, CO_2 = 11.

84

Table 19. Summary of organochlorine, polybrominated diphenyl ether, polychlorinated biphenyl (μg/kg wet weight), and mercury (mg/kg dry weight) concentrations in composite fish samples from the lower Duwamish River (LDR), Lake Washington (LW), and Puget Sound (PS), Washington, 2007.

[Chlorothalonil, dacthal, Di-TCP not detected in any fish composite samples, ND = not detected]

Parameter	Fish Collection Location / Fish Species[1]									
	LW PM	LDR ES	LDR PS	LDR SP	LDR SF	LDR PP	PS ES	PS PS	Age 2-3+ SAL	Age 1 SAL
Wet Weight	4.62	4.63	4.61	4.60	4.60	4.61	4.64	4.60	4.60	4.60
% Lipids	10.80	0.89	1.47	2.82	0.37	1.64	1.61	0.85	3.15	6.86
% Moisture	70.53	82.32	80.25	75.95	81.91	77.33	78.78	80.67	76.55	45.52
1245TCB	ND	ND	ND	ND	ND	ND	ND	ND	ND	ND
1234TCB	0.06	0.02	0.02	0.02	0.02	0.02	0.08	0.12	0.11	0.05
QCB	1.06	0.03	0.37	0.05	0.02	0.04	0.04	0.03	0.06	0.10
HCB	2.46	0.27	0.50	0.58	0.09	0.48	0.20	0.14	0.46	0.41
OCS	0.12	0.07	0.17	0.37	0.02	0.28	0.01	0.02	0.02	0.07
p,p'-DDE	120.74	11.35	6.25	27.39	1.53	7.57	2.07	2.47	3.76	11.37
p,p'-DDD	35.33	3.91	1.26	3.88	0.30	2.58	0.28	0.13	0.43	1.59
p,p'-DDT	0.05	0.70	0.60	1.82	0.18	0.50	0.18	0.16	0.14	0.49
Dieldrin	16.20	0.20	0.24	0.49	0.09	0.33	0.22	0.11	0.27	0.46
Mirex	0.60	0.11	0.04	0.22	0.02	0.10	0.03	0.01	0.01	0.05
trans-Nonachlor	27.70	2.50	1.90	3.61	0.31	1.81	0.67	0.71	0.86	0.91
oxyChlordane	2.39	0.11	0.21	0.47	0.05	0.40	0.08	0.07	0.10	0.32
trans-Chlordane	6.57	0.33	0.20	0.49	0.07	0.11	0.07	0.02	0.08	0.42
cis-Chlordane	20.20	0.70	0.57	1.43	0.14	0.71	0.28	0.10	0.27	0.38
cis-Nonachlor	15.61	0.70	0.44	1.08	0.12	0.50	0.24	0.15	0.18	0.24
Total Chlordanes	72.46	4.34	3.32	7.09	0.68	3.53	1.33	1.05	1.49	1.74
HE	2.34	0.03	0.04	0.08	0.01	0.07	0.04	0.02	0.07	0.07
α-HCH	0.12	0.04	0.06	0.06	0.01	0.07	0.09	0.04	0.18	0.02
β-HCH	0.83	0.05	0.05	0.08	ND	0.07	0.10	0.04	0.16	0.05
γ-HCH	0.08	0.01	ND	ND	ND	0.01	0.02	0.01	0.05	0.01
BDE17	ND	ND	ND	ND	ND	ND	ND	ND	ND	ND
BDE28	1.39	0.09	0.18	0.37	0.05	0.07	0.09	0.16	0.26	0.15
BDE47	28.00	6.60	8.90	13.00	2.00	4.50	8.00	5.70	4.60	1.00
BDE49	1.90	0.32	0.83	1.50	0.03	0.33	0.10	0.19	0.53	0.14
BDE66	0.12	0.14	ND	0.10	ND	ND	0.06	ND	0.10	0.04
BDE85	ND	ND	ND	ND	ND	ND	ND	ND	ND	ND
BDE99	0.28	2.20	0.05	0.20	0.11	0.04	0.37	0.13	2.00	0.27
BDE100	11.00	2.40	2.20	4.20	0.46	1.30	1.70	1.50	1.10	0.23
BDE138	ND	ND	ND	ND	ND	ND	ND	ND	ND	ND
BDE153	3.40	0.66	0.14	ND	0.04	ND	ND	ND	ND	0.05
BDE154/BB153	4.27	0.95	0.44	0.69	0.15	0.21	0.19	0.18	0.16	0.06
BDE183	0.05	ND	ND	ND	ND	ND	ND	0.34	ND	ND
BDE190	ND	ND	ND	ND	ND	ND	ND	ND	ND	ND
BDE209	ND	ND	ND	ND	ND	ND	ND	ND	ND	ND
ΣPBDE[2]	51.00	13.00	13.00	20.00	2.90	6.50	11.00	8.20	8.90	1.89
BB101	0.18	0.09	0.03	0.12	ND	0.06	ND	0.01	0.01	0.11
HBCD	1.4	ND	ND	0.18	ND	0.17	ND	ND	ND	ND
Hg	0.54	0.17	0.20	0.56	0.18	0.18	0.24	0.20	0.10	0.09

[1]PM = Peamouth, ES = English sole, PS = Pacific staghorn sculpin, SP = Shiner perch, SF = Starry flounder, PP = Pile perch, SAL = salmonids; Age 1 year = geometric mean of Chinook, Coho, and Steelhead hatchery salmonid composites; Age 2–3+ year collected from the PS and were about 304 mm in length.
[2]ΣPBDE = sum of congeners 17, 28, 47, 49, 66, 85, 99, 100, 138, 153, 154/BB153, 183, 190, and 209.

Table 19. Summary of organochlorine, polybrominated diphenyl ether, polychlorinated biphenyl (µg/kg wet weight), and mercury (mg/kg dry weight) concentrations in composite fish samples from the lower Duwamish River (LDR), Lake Washington (LW), and Puget Sound (PS), Washington, 2007.—Continued

Parameter	LW PM	LDR ES	LDR PS	LDR SP	LDR SF	LDR PP	PS ES	PS PS	Age 2-3+ SAL	Age 1 SAL
PCB31/28	1.73	3.21	2 22	5.08	0.75	4.07	0 16	0.11	0.45	0.47
PCB42	0.91	3.28	1.17	0 18	0.02	0.05	0.03	0.06	0.08	0.06
PCB44	1.70	2.16	2.43	3.45	0.06	1.07	0.05	0.10	0.27	0.19
PCB49	1.96	8.45	6.02	7.01	0.82	7.80	0.13	0.17	0.28	0.32
PCB52	3.75	10.47	8.74	12.17	1.53	14.74	0.36	0.36	0.67	0.53
PCB56/60	2.75	6.03	4.02	4 93	0.84	3.32	0.19	0.29	0.29	0.19
PCB64	1.44	3.59	1.83	2.78	0.43	2.59	0.07	0.04	0.14	0.09
PCB66/95	9.65	20 95	13.27	15.27	2.59	9.19	0.36	0.74	1.08	0.74
PCB74	2.18	10.12	3.30	9 52	5.08	7.87	5.42	9.10	1.28	1.60
PCB70/76	2.46	6.47	2.56	5 91	0.90	5.76	0.27	0.18	0.35	0.33
PCB87	4.32	11.28	5.41	10.12	0.12	5.69	0.12	0.34	0.29	0.12
PCB97	3.83	6.52	3.51	3 21	0.15	2.17	0.05	0.34	0.32	0.21
PCB99	6.12	22.22	15.37	29.75	3.30	14.90	1.00	1.33	1.04	0.59
PCB101	14.56	35 21	19.03	39.29	2.73	19.90	0.71	1.49	1.27	0.72
PCB105	2.68	4.45	5.27	11.43	0.95	3.84	0.05	0.32	0.25	0.14
PCB110	16.30	26.36	15.97	17.04	3.17	7.47	0.61	1.07	1.17	0.58
PCB118	15.05	34.94	23.80	63.19	4.60	23.80	1.26	1.68	1.17	0.59
PCB128	5.25	6.65	4.67	10.79	1.03	3.14	0.35	0.47	0.27	0.13
PCB138	36.67	68.73	42.21	118.83	10.53	40.66	2.73	4.52	2.43	1.14
PCB141	4.61	9.70	4.55	7 38	1.05	3.15	0.15	0.41	0.23	0.15
PCB146	5.53	10.82	7.11	19.02	1.68	7.40	0.42	0.88	0.52	0.29
PCB149	16.23	37.35	14.02	14.76	3.56	7.26	0.29	1.86	1.64	0.91
PCB151	5.94	15.78	8.13	17.08	2.32	7.35	0.35	0.89	0.53	0.25
PCB153	35 18	87.78	46.32	147.69	14.65	47.88	3.99	5.94	3.15	1.48
PCB158	2.88	5.74	3.64	9 30	1.00	3.17	0.20	0.37	0.15	0.07
PCB170/190	7.58	14.65	10.23	31.65	3.20	11.11	0.45	0.87	0.35	0.18
PCB171/156	5.90	12.41	7 58	22 97	2.07	7 90	0 33	0.74	0.32	0.09
PCB172	1.87	3.08	1.71	4.37	0.50	1.65	0.09	0.19	0.08	0.04
PCB174	4.91	10 59	2.62	1.26	0.82	0.63	0.04	0.40	0.32	0.20
PCB177	4.99	9.61	5 11	11.25	0.95	4.32	0 11	0.67	0.32	0.16
PCB178	2.38	4.50	2.81	5 22	0.66	2.15	0.16	0.43	0.12	0.11
PCB179	2.53	6.95	2.65	3 91	0.78	1.41	0.14	0.29	0.21	0.11
PCB180	22.52	44.77	26.19	81.20	7.30	27.24	1.45	2.73	0.99	0.56
PCB183	5.08	12.83	6.62	20.66	2.31	7.95	0.63	0.90	0.43	0.19
PCB187	11.02	26.67	13.84	42.65	4.07	14.86	0.86	2.26	1.04	0.58
PCB194	4.22	7.24	3.88	9.82	1.12	4.01	0.30	0.46	0.15	0.11
PCB195	1.55	2 51	1.62	4.02	0.46	1.49	0.11	0.22	0.05	0.03
PCB200	1.23	2 37	1.18	3.45	0.32	1.24	0.08	0.16	0.07	0.02
PCB201	4.04	7.70	3.39	7.43	1.14	3.59	0.34	0.60	0.27	0.16
PCB203	5.79	10.60	5.22	14.47	1.71	5.65	0.53	0.66	0.26	0.15
PCB206	1.47	1.96	0.76	2 11	0.30	1.00	0.23	0.20	0.08	0.05
ΣPCBs	290.75	636.69	359.97	851.57	91.57	350.44	25.14	44.84	24.33	14.99
Aroclor5460[2]	502.28	941.48	578.19	1,627.83	144.26	556.93	37.42	61.87	33.23	15.57
Aroclor1260	205.63	408.86	239.20	741.58	66.67	248.74	13.26	24.95	9.08	5.11

[1]PM = Peamouth, ES = English sole, PS = Pacific staghorn sculpin, SP = Shiner perch, SF = Starry flounder, PP = Pile perch, SAL = salmonids; Age 1 year = geometric mean of Chinook, Coho, and Steelhead hatchery salmonid composites; Age 2–3+ year collected from the PS and were about 304 mm in length.
[2]Aroclor1254:1260.

Table 20. Residue concentrations (µg/kg wet weight) in osprey eggs (geometric means) and fish families (whole body) (determined by weighting fish residues by percentage of each fish species biomass in the osprey diet) from the lower Duwamish River (LDR) and adjacent Puget Sound (PS) locations in 2006–07 and associated wet weight biomagnification factors (BMFs: fish to osprey egg).

| Parameter[2] | Osprey Egg[3] | Fish family (% biomass in diet)[1] | | | | | | BMFs |
		CM (8.2)	SUR (13.0)	BC[4] (9.4)	REF[4] (7.7)	SAL (57.1)	OTH[4] (4.6)	
% Lipid[5]	4.14	10.8	1.66	10.8	0.87	6.38	2.67	
PCB31/28	2.39	1.73	4.08	1.73	0.51	0.46	0.96	2.0
PCB44	0.08	1.70	1.10	1.70	0.06	0.20	0.89	0.1
PCB49	3.34	1.96	7.79	1.96	0.54	0.31	1.93	2.0
PCB52	1.85	3.75	14.71	3.75	1.06	0.55	2.99	0.6
PCB56/60	0.19	2.75	3.34	2.75	0.58	0.21	1.36	0.2
PCB64	1.21	1.44	2.59	1.44	0.29	0.10	0.63	1.7
PCB66/95	5.4	9.65	9.27	9.65	1.70	0.78	4.59	1.5
PCB74	2.94	2.18	7.89	2.18	5.22	1.56	1.65	1.1
PCB70/76	1.28	2.46	5.76	2.46	0.65	0.33	1.80	0.9
PCB97	1.86	3.83	2.18	3.83	0.11	0.22	1.23	1.6
PCB99	24.98	6.12	15.10	6.12	2.37	0.64	5.16	6.5
PCB101[6]	32.77	14.56	20.15	14.56	1.92	0.79	6.38	5.4
PCB110	13.11	16.30	7.60	16.30	2.14	0.66	5.43	2.8
PCB118	40.51	15.05	24.31	15.05	3.26	0.66	7.69	6.0
PCB128	13.49	5.25	3.23	5.25	0.75	0.15	1.54	8.7
PCB138	121.98	36.67	41.67	36.67	7.40	1.30	13.88	8.8
PCB141	14.65	4.61	3.21	4.61	0.69	0.16	1.48	10.2
PCB146	26.34	5.53	7.55	5.53	1.17	0.32	2.42	11.3
PCB149	26.24	16.23	7.35	16.23	2.25	1.00	5.20	5.5
PCB151	0.42	5.94	7.48	5.94	1.53	0.29	2.72	0.2
PCB153	149.26	35.18	49.17	35.18	10.37	1.70	15.58	9.9
PCB158	9.86	2.88	3.25	2.88	0.68	0.08	1.15	9.1
PCB171/156	18.78	5.90	8.10	5.90	1.37	0.12	2.51	7.9
PCB172	5.04	1.87	1.69	1.87	0.34	0.05	0.55	8.1
PCB174	8.85	4.91	0.64	4.91	0.51	0.21	0.98	7.7
PCB177	16.14	4.99	4.41	4.99	0.61	0.18	1.70	9.6
PCB180	107.71	22.52	27.94	22.52	4.95	0.62	8.25	12.4
PCB183	27.79	5.08	8.12	5.08	1.63	0.22	2.21	12.1
PCB187[6]	56.03	11.02	15.23	11.02	2.78	0.64	4.72	11.9
PCB194	22.41	4.22	4.09	4.22	0.79	0.11	1.22	15.4
PCB195	6.45	1.55	1.52	1.55	0.32	0.03	0.50	12.1
PCB201	20.63	4.04	3.64	4.04	0.82	0.17	1.16	14.8
PCB203[6]	24.79	5.79	5.76	5.79	1.24	0.17	1.69	12.2
PCB206	6.02	1.47	1.02	1.47	0.27	0.06	0.27	13.2
ΣPCB	897.02	290.75	356.95	290.75	64.86	16.20	120.99	7.6
BDE28	4.3	1.39	0.07	1.39	0.07	0.16	0.24	11.8
BDE47	161.64	28.00	4.58	28.00	4.43	1.46	5.80	23.3
BDE49	0.17	1.90	0.34	1.90	0.06	0.19	0.61	0.3
BDE66	1.61	0.12	0.00	0.12	0.02	0.05	0.09	28.9
BDE99	39.91	0.28	0.04	0.28	0.22	0.50	1.46	94.3
BDE100	46.17	11.00	1.32	11.00	0.94	0.34	1.43	18.9
BDE153	16.97	3.40	0.00	3.40	0.03	0.04	0.04	27.1
BDE154/BB153	19.17	4.27	0.22	4.27	0.16	0.07	0.24	22.7

Table 20. Residue concentrations (µg/kg wet weight) in osprey eggs (geometric means) and fish families (whole body) (determined by weighting fish residues by percentage of each fish species biomass in the osprey diet) from the lower Duwamish River (LDR) and adjacent Puget Sound (PS) locations in 2006–07 and associated wet weight biomagnification factors (BMFs: fish to osprey egg).—Continued

| | | Fish family (% biomass in diet)[1] | | | | | | |
Parameter[2]	Osprey Egg[3]	CM (8.2)	SUR (13.0)	BC[4] (9.4)	REF[4] (7.7)	SAL (57.1)	OTH[4] (4.6)	BMFs
ΣPBDE	320.89	51.00	6.66	51.00	6.07	2.81	10.02	25.9
QCB	0.32	1.06	0.04	1.06	0.03	0.09	0.15	1.3
HCB	1.15	2.46	0.48	2.46	0.13	0.42	0.47	1.5
p,p'-DDE	142.99	120.74	7.83	120.74	1.75	10.38	4.48	5.0
p,p'-DDD	24.43	35.33	2.60	35.33	0.29	1.44	0.67	3.3
p,p'-DDT	1.97	0.05	0.52	0.05	0.18	0.44	0.27	5.6
Dieldrin	0.97	16.20	0.33	16.20	0.14	0.43	0.26	0.3
Mirex	2.35	0.60	0.10	0.60	0.02	0.04	0.02	16.2
Total chlordanes	13.61	72.46	3.57	72.46	0.94	1.71	2.02	0.9
HE	2.24	2.34	0.07	2.34	0.02	0.07	0.06	4.8
β-HCH	0.79	0.83	0.07	0.83	0.04	0.07	0.13	3.9

[1]CM = carp and minnows: peamouth (1 composite [C]: 7 fish [F]); SUR = surfperches: pile perch (1C: 2F), shiner perch (1C: 7F); BC = bullheads and catfish: bullheads (peamouth residue data used); REF = righteye flounder: LDR starry flounder (SF) (1C: 3F), PS SF (LDR SF residue data used), PS English sole (1C: 7F); SAL = salmonids: Soos Creek hatchery (SCH) steelhead (1C: 7F), SCH chinook (1C: 7F), SCH coho (1C: 7F), PS chinook (1C: 2F); OTH = other: smelts (PS salmonid data used), PS Pacific staghorn sculpin (1C: 4F).

[2]PCB = polychlorinated biphenyl, BDE = brominated diphenyl ether, PBDE = polybrominated diphenyl ethers, QCB = pentachlorobenzene, HCB = hexachlorobenzene, total chlordanes = sum of *trans*-nonachlor, *cis*-nonachlor, oxychlordane, *trans*-chlordane, and *cis*-chlordane, HE = heptachlor epoxide, β-HCH = beta-hexachlorocyclohexane.

[3](N=11) collected from nests along the LDR.

[4]Contains surrogate residue data, see footnote 1.

[5]Percent lipid calculated using proportions observed in diet (pre-incubation period) when family category consisted of multiple species.

[6]Osprey egg congeners coelueted (PCB101: congeners 101 + 90, PCB187: congeners 182 + 187: PCB203: congeners 203+196).